MznLnx

Missing Links Exam Preps

Exam Prep for

Geometry

Jurgensen & Brown, 5th Edition

The MznLnx Exam Prep is your link from the texbook and lecture to your exams.
The MznLnx Exam Preps are unauthorized and comprehensive reviews of your textbooks.

All material provided by MznLnx and Rico Publications (c) 2010
Textbook publishers and textbook authors do not particpate in or contribute to these reviews.

MznLnx

Rico
Publications

Exam Prep for Geometry
5th Edition
Jurgensen & Brown

Publisher: Raymond Houge
Assistant Editor: Michael Rouger
Text and Cover Designer: Lisa Buckner
Marketing Manager: Sara Swagger
Project Manager, Editorial Production: Jerry Emerson
Art Director: Vernon Lowerui

Product Manager: Dave Mason
Editorial Assitant: Rachel Guzmanji
Pedagogy: Debra Long
Cover Image: Jim Reed/Getty Images
Text and Cover Printer: City Printing, Inc.
Compositor: Media Mix, Inc.

(c) 2010 Rico Publications
ALL RIGHTS RESERVED. No part of this work covered by the copyright may be reproduced or used in any form or by an means--graphic, electronic, or mechanical, including photocopying, recording, taping, Web distribution, information storage, and retrieval systems, or in any other manner--without the written permission of the publisher.

For more information about our products, contact us at:

Dave.Mason@RicoPublications.com

For permission to use material from this text or

product, submit a request online to:

Dave.Mason@RicoPublications.com

Printed in the United States
ISBN:

Contents

CHAPTER 1
POINTS, LINES, PLANES, AND ANGLES — 1

CHAPTER 2
DEDUCTIVE REASONING — 9

CHAPTER 3
PARALLEL LINES AND PLANES — 15

CHAPTER 4
CONGRUENT TRIANGLES — 25

CHAPTER 5
QUADRILATERALS — 32

CHAPTER 6
INEQUALITIES IN GEOMETRY — 39

CHAPTER 7
SIMILAR POLYGONS — 47

CHAPTER 8
RIGHT TRIANGLES — 56

CHAPTER 9
CIRCLES — 63

CHAPTER 10
CONSTRUCTIONS AND LOCI — 69

CHAPTER 11
AREAS OF PLANE FIGURES — 77

CHAPTER 12
AREAS AND VOLUMES OF SOLIDS — 86

CHAPTER 13
COORDINATE GEOMETRY — 93

CHAPTER 14
TRANSFORMATIONS — 100

ANSWER KEY — 111

TO THE STUDENT

COMPREHENSIVE

The *MznLnx* Exam Prep series is designed to help you pass your exams. Editors at MznLnx review your textbooks and then prepare these practice exams to help you master the textbook material. Unlike study guides, workbooks, and practice tests provided by the texbook publisher and textbook authors, *MznLnx* gives you **all** of the material in each chapter in exam form, not just samples, so you can be sure to nail your exam.

MECHANICAL

The MznLnx Exam Prep series creates exams that will help you learn the subject matter as well as test you on your understanding. Each question is designed to help you master the concept. Just working through the exams, you gain an understanding of the subject--its a simple mechanical process that produces success.

INTEGRATED STUDY GUIDE AND REVIEW

MznLnx is not just a set of exams designed to test you, its also a comprehensive review of the subject content. Each exam question is also a review of the concept, making sure that you will get the answer correct without having to go to other sources of material. You learn as you go! Its the easiest way to pass an exam.

HUMOR

Studying can be tedious and dry. MznLnx's instructional design includes moderate humor within the exam questions on occassion, to break the tedium and revitalize the brain

Chapter 1. POINTS, LINES, PLANES, AND ANGLES   1

1. In mathematics, a _____ is a flat surface. _____s can arise as subspaces of some higher dimensional space, as with the walls of a room, or they may enjoy an independent existence in their own right, as in the setting of Euclidean geometry
    a. Pendent
    b. Simple polytope
    c. Plane
    d. Parallelogram law

2. In geometry, topology and related branches of mathematics a spatial _____ describes a specific object within a given space that consists of neither volume, area, length, nor any other higher dimensional analogue. Thus, a _____ is a 0-dimensional object. Because of their nature as one of the simplest geometric concepts, they are often used in one form or another as the fundamental constituents of geometry, physics, vector graphics, and many other fields.
    a. 1-center problem
    b. -module
    c. Point
    d. 11-cell

3. _____ is the boundless, three-dimensional extent in which objects and events occur and have relative position and direction. Physical _____ is often conceived in three linear dimensions, although modern physicists usually consider it, with time, to be part of the boundless four-dimensional continuum known as spacetime. In mathematics _____s with different numbers of dimensions and with different underlying structures can be examined.
    a. Space
    b. 11-cell
    c. 1-center problem
    d. -module

4. In geometry, a set of points in space is _____ if the points all lie in the same geometric plane. For example, three distinct points are always _____; but four points in space are usually not _____.

Points can be shown to be _____ by determining that the scalar product of a vector that is normal to the plane and a vector from any point on the plane to the point being tested is 0.

    a. Minimum bounding box
    b. Coordinate geometry
    c. Quantum torus
    d. Coplanar

5. A _____ is a building where the outer surfaces are triangular and converge at a point. The base of a _____ is usually trilateral or quadrilateral (but may be of any polygon shape), meaning that a _____ usually has four or five faces. A _____'s design, with the majority of the weight closer to the ground, means that less material higher up on the _____ will be pushing down from above: this allowed early civilizations to create stable monumental structures.
    a. -module
    b. 1-center problem
    c. 11-cell
    d. Pyramid

6. A pair of angles is said to be _____ or opposite if the angles share the same vertex and are bounded by the same pair of lines but are opposite to each other. Such angles are congruent and thus have equal measure. If two line segments, EF and GH, intersect at the point P, they form four angles, EPG, GPF, FPH, and HPE.
    a. Conway polyhedron notation
    b. Vertical
    c. Mirror image
    d. Complementary angles

Chapter 1. POINTS, LINES, PLANES, AND ANGLES

7. A timeline of _____ and geometry

- ca. 2000 BC -- Scotland, Carved Stone Balls exhibit a variety of symmetries including all of the symmetries of Platonic solids.
- 1800 BC -- Moscow Mathematical Papyrus, findings volume of a frustum
- 1650 BC -- Rhind Mathematical Papyrus, copy of a lost scroll from around 1850 BC, the scribe Ahmes presents one of the first known approximate values of π at 3.16, the first attempt at squaring the circle, earliest known use of a sort of cotangent, and knowledge of solving first order linear equations
- 1300 BC -- Berlin papyrus (19th dynasty) contains a quadratic equation and its solution.

- 800 BC -- Baudhayana, author of the Baudhayana Sulba Sutra, a Vedic Sanskrit geometric text, contains quadratic equations, and calculates the square root of 2 correct to five decimal places
- ca. 600 BC -- the other Vedic 'Sulba Sutras' use Pythagorean triples, contain of a number of geometrical proofs, and approximate π at 3.16
- 5th century BC -- Hippocrates of Chios utilizes lunes in an attempt to square the circle
- 5th century BC -- Apastamba, author of the Apastamba Sulba Sutra, another Vedic Sanskrit geometric text, makes an attempt at squaring the circle and also calculates the square root of 2 correct to five decimal places
- 530 BC -- Pythagoras studies propositional geometry and vibrating lyre strings; his group also discover the irrationality of the square root of two,
- 370 BC -- Eudoxus states the method of exhaustion for area determination
- 300 BC -- Euclid in his Elements studies geometry as an axiomatic system, proves the infinitude of prime numbers and presents the Euclidean algorithm; he states the law of reflection in Catoptrics, and he proves the fundamental theorem of arithmetic
- 260 BC -- Archimedes proved that the value of π lies between 3 + 1/7 and 3 + 10/71 (approx. 3.1408), that the area of a circle was equal to π multiplied by the square of the radius of the circle and that the area enclosed by a parabola and a straight line is 4/3 multiplied by the area of a triangle with equal base and height. He also gave a very accurate estimate of the value of the square root of 3.
- 225 BC -- Apollonius of Perga writes On Conic Sections and names the ellipse, parabola, and hyperbola,
- 150 BC -- Jain mathematicians in India write the 'Sthananga Sutra', which contains work on the theory of numbers, arithmetical operations, geometry, operations with fractions, simple equations, cubic equations, quartic equations, and permutations and combinations
- 140 BC -- Hipparchus develops the bases of trigonometry.

- 1st century -- Heron of Alexandria, the earliest fleeting reference to square roots of negative numbers.
- 250 -- Diophantus uses symbols for unknown numbers in terms of syncopated _____, and writes Arithmetica, one of the earliest treatises on _____
- ca. 340 -- Pappus of Alexandria states his hexagon theorem and his centroid theorem
- 500 -- Aryabhata writes the 'Aryabhata-Siddhanta', which first introduces the trigonometric functions and methods of calculating their approximate numerical values. It defines the concepts of sine and cosine, and also contains the earliest tables of sine and cosine values
- 600s -- Bhaskara I gives a rational approximation of the sine function
- 600s -- Brahmagupta invents the method of solving indeterminate equations of the second degree and is the first to use _____ to solve astronomical problems. He also develops methods for calculations of the motions and places of various planets, their rising and setting, conjunctions, and the calculation of eclipses of the sun and the moon
- 628 -- Brahmagupta writes the Brahma-sphuta-siddhanta, where zero is clearly explained, and where the modern place-value Indian numeral system is fully developed. It also gives rules for manipulating both negative and positive numbers, methods for computing square roots, methods of solving linear and quadratic equations, and rules for summing series, Brahmagupta's identity, and the Brahmagupta theorem
- 700s -- Virasena gives explicit rules for the Fibonacci sequence, gives the derivation of the volume of a frustum using an infinite procedure, and also deals with the logarithm to base 2 and knows its laws
- 700s -- Shridhara gives the rule for finding the volume of a sphere and also the formula for solving quadratic equations
- 820 -- Al-Khwarizmi -- Persian mathematician, father of _____, writes the Al-Jabr, later transliterated as _____, which introduces systematic algebraic techniques for solving linear and quadratic equations. Translations of his book on arithmetic will introduce the Hindu-Arabic decimal number system to the Western world in the 12th century.

The term algorithm is also named after him.
- 820 -- Al-Mahani conceived the idea of reducing geometrical problems such as doubling the cube to problems in _____.
- 895 -- Thabit ibn Qurra: the only surviving fragment of his original work contains a chapter on the solution and properties of cubic equations. He also generalized the Pythagorean theorem, and discovered the theorem by which pairs of amicable numbers can be found, .
- ca. 900 -- Abu Kamil of Egypt had begun to understand what we would write in symbols as $x^n \cdot x^m = x^{m+n}$
- 953 -- Al-Karaji is the 'first person to completely free _____ from geometrical operations and to replace them with the arithmetical type of operations which are at the core of _____ today. He was first to define the monomials x, x^2, x^3, … and 1 / x, 1 / x^2, 1 / x^3, … and to give rules for products of any two of these. He started a school of _____ which flourished for several hundreds of years'. He also discovered the binomial theorem for integer exponents, which 'was a major factor in the development of numerical analysis based on the decimal system.'
- 975 -- Al-Batani -- Extended the Indian concepts of sine and cosine to other trigonometrical ratios, like tangent, secant and their inverse functions. Derived the formula: $\sin \alpha = \tan \alpha / \sqrt{1 + \tan^2 \alpha}$ and $\cos \alpha = 1 / \sqrt{1 + \tan^2 \alpha}$.
- ca. 1000 -- Abū Sahl al-Qūhī (Kuhi) solves equations higher than the second degree.
- ca. 1000 -- Law of sines is discovered by Muslim mathematicians, but it is uncertain who discovers it first between Abu-Mahmud al-Khujandi, Abu Nasr Mansur, and Abu al-Wafa.
- 1070 -- Omar Khayyám begins to write Treatise on Demonstration of Problems of _____ and classifies cubic equations.
- ca. 1100 -- Omar Khayyám 'gave a complete classification of cubic equations with geometric solutions found by means of intersecting conic sections.' He became the first to find general geometric solutions of cubic equations and laid the foundations for the development of analytic geometry and non-Euclidean geometry. He also extracted roots using the decimal system .
- 1100s -- Bhaskara Acharya writes the 'Bijaganita' , which is the first text that recognizes that a positive number has two square roots
- 1130 -- Al-Samawal gave a definition of _____: '[it is concerned] with operating on unknowns using all the arithmetical tools, in the same way as the arithmetician operates on the known.'
- 1135 -- Sharafeddin Tusi followed al-Khayyam's application of _____ to geometry, and wrote a treatise on cubic equations which 'represents an essential contribution to another _____ which aimed to study curves by means of equations, thus inaugurating the beginning of algebraic geometry.'
- ca. 1250 -- Nasir Al-Din Al-Tusi attempts to develop a form of non-Euclidean geometry.
- 1400s -- Nilakantha Somayaji, a Kerala school mathematician, writes the 'Aryabhatiya Bhasya', which contains work on infinite-series expansions, problems of _____, and spherical geometry

- 1520 -- Scipione dal Ferro develops a method for solving 'depressed' cubic equations (cubic equations without an x^2 term), but does not publish.
- 1535 -- Niccolo Tartaglia independently develops a method for solving depressed cubic equations but also does not publish.
- 1539 -- Gerolamo Cardano learns Tartaglia's method for solving depressed cubics and discovers a method for depressing cubics, thereby creating a method for solving all cubics.
- 1540 -- Lodovico Ferrari solves the quartic equation.

- 1600s - Putumana Somayaji writes the 'Paddhati', which presents a detailed discussion of various trigonometric series
- 1619 - René Descartes discovers analytic geometry (Pierre de Fermat claimed that he also discovered it independently),
- 1619 - Johannes Kepler discovers two of the Kepler-Poinsot polyhedra.
- 1637 - Pierre de Fermat claims to have proven Fermat's Last Theorem in his copy of Diophantus' Arithmetica,
- 1637 - First use of the term imaginary number by René Descartes; it was meant to be derogatory.

- 1722 - Abraham de Moivre states de Moivre's formula connecting trigonometric functions and complex numbers,
- 1733 - Giovanni Gerolamo Saccheri studies what geometry would be like if Euclid's fifth postulate were false,
- 1796 - Carl Friedrich Gauss proves that the regular 17-gon can be constructed using only a compass and straightedge
- 1797 - Caspar Wessel associates vectors with complex numbers and studies complex number operations in geometrical terms,
- 1799 - Carl Friedrich Gauss proves the fundamental theorem of _____,

- 1799 - Paolo Ruffini partially proves the Abel-Ruffini theorem that quintic or higher equations cannot be solved by a general formula,

- 1806 - Louis Poinsot discovers the two remaining Kepler-Poinsot polyhedra.
- 1806 - Jean-Robert Argand publishes proof of the Fundamental theorem of _____ and the Argand diagram,
- 1824 - Niels Henrik Abel partially proves the Abel-Ruffini theorem that the general quintic or higher equations cannot be solved by a general formula involving only arithmetical operations and roots,
- 1829 - Bolyai, Gauss, and Lobachevsky invent hyperbolic non-Euclidean geometry,
- 1832 - Évariste Galois presents a general condition for the solvability of algebraic equations, thereby essentially founding group theory and Galois theory,
- 1837 - Pierre Wantsel proves that doubling the cube and trisecting the angle are impossible with only a compass and straightedge, as well as the full completion of the problem of constructability of regular polygons
- 1843 - William Hamilton discovers the calculus of quaternions and deduces that they are non-commutative,
- 1847 - George Boole formalizes symbolic logic in The Mathematical Analysis of Logic, defining what now is called Boolean _____,
- 1854 - Bernhard Riemann introduces Riemannian geometry,
- 1854 - Arthur Cayley shows that quaternions can be used to represent rotations in four-dimensional space,
- 1858 - August Ferdinand Möbius invents the Möbius strip,
- 1870 - Felix Klein constructs an analytic geometry for Lobachevski's geometry thereby establishing its self-consistency and the logical independence of Euclid's fifth postulate,
- 1873 - Charles Hermite proves that e is transcendental,
- 1878 - Charles Hermite solves the general quintic equation by means of elliptic and modular functions
- 1882 - Ferdinand von Lindemann proves that π is transcendental and that therefore the circle cannot be squared with a compass and straightedge,
- 1882 - Felix Klein invents the Klein bottle,
- 1899 - David Hilbert presents a set of self-consistent geometric axioms in Foundations of Geometry,

- 1901 - Élie Cartan develops the exterior derivative,
- 1905 - Einstein's theory of special relativity.
- 1912 - Luitzen Egbertus Jan Brouwer presents the Brouwer fixed-point theorem,
- 1916 - Einstein's theory of general relativity.
- 1930 - Casimir Kuratowski shows that the three-cottage problem has no solution,
- 1931 - Georges de Rham develops theorems in cohomology and characteristic classes,
- 1933 - Karol Borsuk and Stanislaw Ulam present the Borsuk-Ulam antipodal-point theorem,
- 1955 - H. S. M. Coxeter et al. publish the complete list of uniform polyhedron,
- 1981 - Mikhail Gromov develops the theory of hyperbolic groups, revolutionizing both infinite group theory and global differential geometry,
- 1983 - the classification of finite simple groups, a collaborative work involving some hundred mathematicians and spanning thirty years, is completed,
- 1991 - Alain Connes and John W. Lott develop non-commutative geometry,
- 1998 - Thomas Callister Hales (almost certainly) proves the Kepler conjecture,

- 2003 - Grigori Perelman proves the Poincaré conjecture,
- 2007 - a team of researches throughout North America and Europe used networks of computers to map E8 (mathematics.)

Chapter 1. POINTS, LINES, PLANES, AND ANGLES

a. ADHM construction
b. ADE classification
c. AA postulate
d. Algebra

8. In each statement above, a is not equal to b. These relations are known as strict _____. The notation a < b may also be read as 'a is strictly less than b'.

a. AA postulate
b. ADE classification
c. Inequalities
d. ADHM construction

9. In chemistry, the _____ molecular geometry describes the arrangement of three or more atoms placed at an expected bond angle of 180Å°. _____ organic molecules, e.g. acetylene, are often described by invoking sp orbital hybridization for the carbon centers. Many _____ molecules exist, prominent examples include CO_2, HCN, and xenon difluoride.

a. Linear
b. -module
c. 11-cell
d. 1-center problem

10. where a is any scalar. A function which satisfies these properties is called a linear function, or more generally a linear map. This property makes _____s particularly easy to solve and reason about.

a. 1-center problem
b. -module
c. 11-cell
d. Linear equation

11. In mathematics, the _____ of a real number is its numerical value without regard to its sign. So, for example, 3 is the _____ of both 3 and −3.

The _____ of a number a is denoted by | a |.

a. ADHM construction
b. ADE classification
c. AA postulate
d. Absolute value

12. A _____ is a number that determines the location of a point along some line or curve. A list of two, three, or more _____s can be used to determine the location of a point on a surface, volume, or higher-dimensional domain.

For example, the longitude is a _____ which determines the position of a point along the Earth's equator, and latitude is another _____ that defines a poisition along a meridian.

a. 1-center problem
b. -module
c. 11-cell
d. Coordinate

13. Determining the _____ segment--also called rectification of a curve--was historically difficult. Although many methods were used for specific curves, the advent of calculus led to a general formula that provides closed-form solutions in some cases.

a. 1-center problem
b. -module
c. 11-cell
d. Length of an irregular arc

14. In geometry, an _____ is a closed segment of a differentiable curve in the two-dimensional plane; for example, a circular _____ is a segment of the circumference of a circle. If the _____ segment occupies a great circle (or great ellipse), it is considered a great-_____ segment.

The length of an _____ of a circle with radius r and subtending an angle ☐> (measured in radians) with the circle center -- i.e., the central angle -- equals ☐>.

   a. Almost symplectic manifold
   b. Arc
   c. Equiangular polygon
   d. Order-4 dodecahedral honeycomb

15. In the field of mathematical logic, a clear distinction is made between two notions of _____s: logical _____s and non-logical _____s (somewhat similar to the ancient distinction between '_____s' and 'postulates' respectively)

These are certain formulas in a formal language that are universally valid, that is, formulas that are satisfied by every assignment of values. Usually one takes as logical _____s at least some minimal set of tautologies that is sufficient for proving all tautologies in the language; in the case of predicate logic more logical _____s than that are required, in order to prove logical truths that are not tautologies in the strict sense.

In propositional logic it is common to take as logical _____s all formulae of the following forms, where φ, χ, and ψ can be any formulae of the language and where the included primitive connectives are only '¬' for negation of the immediately following proposition and '→' for implication from antecedent to consequent propositions:

1. $\phi \to (\psi \to \phi)$
2. $(\phi \to (\psi \to \chi)) \to ((\phi \to \psi) \to (\phi \to \chi))$
3. $(\neg\phi \to \neg\psi) \to (\psi \to \phi).$

Each of these patterns is an _____ schema, a rule for generating an infinite number of _____s. For example, if A, B, and C are propositional variables, then $A \to (B \to A)$ and $(A \to \neg B) \to (C \to (A \to \neg B))$ are both instances of _____ schema 1, and hence are _____s.

   a. AA postulate
   b. ADE classification
   c. Inductive reasoning
   d. Axiom

16. In the field of mathematical logic, a clear distinction is made between two notions of axioms: _____ and non-_____

Chapter 1. POINTS, LINES, PLANES, AND ANGLES 5

These are certain formulas in a formal language that are universally valid, that is, formulas that are satisfied by every assignment of values. Usually one takes as _____ at least some minimal set of tautologies that is sufficient for proving all tautologies in the language; in the case of predicate logic more _____ than that are required, in order to prove logical truths that are not tautologies in the strict sense.

In propositional logic it is common to take as _____ all formulae of the following forms, where φ, χ, and ψ can be any formulae of the language and where the included primitive connectives are only '¬' for negation of the immediately following proposition and '⟶' for implication from antecedent to consequent propositions:

1. $\phi \to (\psi \to \phi)$
2. $(\phi \to (\psi \to \chi)) \to ((\phi \to \psi) \to (\phi \to \chi))$
3. $(\neg \phi \to \neg \psi) \to (\psi \to \phi)$.

Each of these patterns is an axiom schema, a rule for generating an infinite number of axioms. For example, if A, B, and C are propositional variables, then $A \to (B \to A)$ and $(A \to \neg B) \to (C \to (A \to \neg B))$ are both instances of axiom schema 1, and hence are axioms.

- a. Contrapositive
- b. Theorem
- c. Logical axioms
- d. Logically equivalent

17. In geometry, two sets of points are called _____ if one can be transformed into the other by an isometry, i.e., a combination of translations, rotations and reflections. Less formally, two figures are _____ if they have the same shape and size, but are in different positions (for instance one may be rotated, flipped, or simply placed somewhere else).
    - a. -module
    - b. Congruent
    - c. 1-center problem
    - d. 11-cell

18. The _____ is the middle point of a line segment. It is equidistant from both endpoints. The formula for determining the _____ of a segment in the plane, with endpoints and is

$$\left(\frac{x_1 + x_2}{2}, \frac{y_1 + y_2}{2} \right).$$

In three-dimensional Cartesian space, the _____ formula is

$$\left(\frac{x_1 + x_2}{2}, \frac{y_1 + y_2}{2}, \frac{z_1 + z_2}{2} \right).$$

_____ used in algebra 1=rectangles _____ used in algebra 2=triangles _____ used in geometry=circles

- Astrology _____ s
- Median
- Segment bisector
- Numerical Integration

a. Midpoint
b. Parallel postulate
c. Quincunx
d. Golden angle

19. In geometry and trigonometry, an _____ is the figure formed by two rays sharing a common endpoint, called the vertex of the _____ . The magnitude of the _____ is the 'amount of rotation' that separates the two rays, and can be measured by considering the length of circular arc swept out when one ray is rotated about the vertex to coincide with the other Where there is no possibility of confusion, the term '_____' is used interchangeably for both the geometric configuration itself and for its angular magnitude (which is simply a numerical quantity.)

a. AA postulate
b. Angle
c. ADE classification
d. ADHM construction

20. In geometry, a _____ is a circular or semicircular tool for measuring an angle or a circle. The units of measurement utilized are usually degrees.

Some _____ s are simple half-discs; these have existed since ancient times.

a. -module
b. Protractor
c. 11-cell
d. 1-center problem

21. In the geometry of curves a _____ is a point of where the first derivative of curvature is zero. This is typically a local maximum or minimum of curvature. Other special cases may occur, for instance when the second derivative is also zero, or when the curvature is constant.

a. Vertex
b. Non-Euclidean crystallographic group
c. Coordinate-induced basis
d. Holomorphic vector bundle

22. In geometry and trigonometry, a _____ is an angle of 90 degrees, corresponding to a quarter turn (that is, a quarter of a full circle.) It can be defined; as the angle such that twice that angle amounts to a half turn, or 180°.

Lines that are at a _____ to each other are perpendicular, an important geometrical property.

a. 1-center problem
b. Right Angle
c. Trigonometric
d. -module

23. In geometry, bisection is the division of something into two equal or congruent parts, usually by a line, which is then called a bisector. The most often considered types of bisectors are segment bisectors and _____ . Bisection of a line segment using a compass and ruler Bisection of an angle using a compass and ruler

Chapter 1. POINTS, LINES, PLANES, AND ANGLES

a. Axis of symmetry
b. Annulus
c. Inscribed sphere
d. Angle bisectors

24. _____ is an adjective meaning contiguous, adjoining or abutting.

In geometry, _____ is when sides meet to make an angle.

In trigonometry the _____ side of a right angled triangle is the cathetus next to the angle in question.

a. Adjacent
b. Equidimensional
c. Ambient space
d. Edge figure

25. In geometry, _____ are angles that have a common ray coming out of the vertex going between two other rays. In other words, they are angles that are side by side, or adjacent.

a. ADE classification
b. AA postulate
c. Elliptic geometry
d. Adjacent angles

26. A _____ is one of the basic shapes of geometry: a polygon with three corners or vertices and three sides or edges which are line segments. A _____ with vertices A, B, and C is denoted ABC.

In Euclidean geometry any three non-collinear points determine a unique _____ and a unique plane (i.e. a two-dimensional Euclidean space.)

a. 11-cell
b. -module
c. Triangle
d. 1-center problem

27. In mathematics and logic, the phrase 'there is _____' is used to indicate that exactly one object with a certain property exists. In mathematical logic, this sort of quantification is known as uniqueness quantification or unique existential quantification.

Uniqueness quantification is often denoted with the symbols '∃!' or $∃_{=1}$'.

a. AA postulate
b. ADHM construction
c. One and only one
d. ADE classification

28. In mathematics and logic, the phrase 'there is one and only one' is used to indicate that exactly one object with a certain property exists. In mathematical logic, this sort of quantification is known as _____ quantification or unique existential quantification.

_____ quantification is often denoted with the symbols '∃!' or $∃_{=1}$'.

a. ADHM construction
b. ADE classification
c. AA postulate
d. Uniqueness

29. An _____ describes the structure and behaviour of applications used in a business, focused on how they interact with each other and with users. It is focused on the data consumed and produced by applications rather than their internal structure. In application portfolio management, the applications are usually mapped to business functions and to application platform technologies.
   a. ADHM construction
   b. Applications architecture
   c. ADE classification
   d. AA postulate

Chapter 2. DEDUCTIVE REASONING

1. In logic, and especially in its applications to mathematics and philosophy, a _____ is an exception to a proposed general rule. For example, consider the proposition 'all students are lazy'. Because this statement makes the claim that a certain property (laziness) holds for all students, even a single example of a diligent student will prove it false.
   - a. 1-center problem
   - b. Corollary
   - c. -module
   - d. Counterexample

2. In computer science, _____s, conditional expressions and conditional constructs are features of a programming language which perform different computations or actions depending on whether a programmer-specified condition evaluates to true or false Apart from the case of branch predication, this is always achieved by selectively altering the control flow based on some condition.

   In imperative programming languages, the term '_____' is usually used, whereas in functional programming, the terms 'conditional expression' or 'conditional construct' are preferred, because these terms all have distinct meanings.

   - a. -module
   - b. 1-center problem
   - c. 11-cell
   - d. Conditional statement

3. In logic and mathematics, logical _____ is a logical operator connecting two statements to assert, p if and only if q where p is a hypothesis and q is a conclusion The operator is denoted using a doubleheaded arrow '↔', an equality sign '=', an equivalence sign '≡', or EQV. It is logically equivalent to ∧, or the XNOR boolean operator.
   - a. Rule of inference
   - b. Logical axioms
   - c. Theorem
   - d. Biconditional

Chapter 2. DEDUCTIVE REASONING

4. A timeline of _____ and geometry

- ca. 2000 BC -- Scotland, Carved Stone Balls exhibit a variety of symmetries including all of the symmetries of Platonic solids.
- 1800 BC -- Moscow Mathematical Papyrus, findings volume of a frustum
- 1650 BC -- Rhind Mathematical Papyrus, copy of a lost scroll from around 1850 BC, the scribe Ahmes presents one of the first known approximate values of π at 3.16, the first attempt at squaring the circle, earliest known use of a sort of cotangent, and knowledge of solving first order linear equations
- 1300 BC -- Berlin papyrus (19th dynasty) contains a quadratic equation and its solution.

- 800 BC -- Baudhayana, author of the Baudhayana Sulba Sutra, a Vedic Sanskrit geometric text, contains quadratic equations, and calculates the square root of 2 correct to five decimal places
- ca. 600 BC -- the other Vedic 'Sulba Sutras' use Pythagorean triples, contain of a number of geometrical proofs, and approximate π at 3.16
- 5th century BC -- Hippocrates of Chios utilizes lunes in an attempt to square the circle
- 5th century BC -- Apastamba, author of the Apastamba Sulba Sutra, another Vedic Sanskrit geometric text, makes an attempt at squaring the circle and also calculates the square root of 2 correct to five decimal places
- 530 BC -- Pythagoras studies propositional geometry and vibrating lyre strings; his group also discover the irrationality of the square root of two,
- 370 BC -- Eudoxus states the method of exhaustion for area determination
- 300 BC -- Euclid in his Elements studies geometry as an axiomatic system, proves the infinitude of prime numbers and presents the Euclidean algorithm; he states the law of reflection in Catoptrics, and he proves the fundamental theorem of arithmetic
- 260 BC -- Archimedes proved that the value of π lies between 3 + 1/7 and 3 + 10/71 (approx. 3.1408), that the area of a circle was equal to π multiplied by the square of the radius of the circle and that the area enclosed by a parabola and a straight line is 4/3 multiplied by the area of a triangle with equal base and height. He also gave a very accurate estimate of the value of the square root of 3.
- 225 BC -- Apollonius of Perga writes On Conic Sections and names the ellipse, parabola, and hyperbola,
- 150 BC -- Jain mathematicians in India write the 'Sthananga Sutra', which contains work on the theory of numbers, arithmetical operations, geometry, operations with fractions, simple equations, cubic equations, quartic equations, and permutations and combinations
- 140 BC -- Hipparchus develops the bases of trigonometry.

- 1st century -- Heron of Alexandria, the earliest fleeting reference to square roots of negative numbers.
- 250 -- Diophantus uses symbols for unknown numbers in terms of syncopated _____, and writes Arithmetica, one of the earliest treatises on _____
- ca. 340 -- Pappus of Alexandria states his hexagon theorem and his centroid theorem
- 500 -- Aryabhata writes the 'Aryabhata-Siddhanta', which first introduces the trigonometric functions and methods of calculating their approximate numerical values. It defines the concepts of sine and cosine, and also contains the earliest tables of sine and cosine values
- 600s -- Bhaskara I gives a rational approximation of the sine function
- 600s -- Brahmagupta invents the method of solving indeterminate equations of the second degree and is the first to use _____ to solve astronomical problems. He also develops methods for calculations of the motions and places of various planets, their rising and setting, conjunctions, and the calculation of eclipses of the sun and the moon
- 628 -- Brahmagupta writes the Brahma-sphuta-siddhanta, where zero is clearly explained, and where the modern place-value Indian numeral system is fully developed. It also gives rules for manipulating both negative and positive numbers, methods for computing square roots, methods of solving linear and quadratic equations, and rules for summing series, Brahmagupta's identity, and the Brahmagupta theorem
- 700s -- Virasena gives explicit rules for the Fibonacci sequence, gives the derivation of the volume of a frustum using an infinite procedure, and also deals with the logarithm to base 2 and knows its laws
- 700s -- Shridhara gives the rule for finding the volume of a sphere and also the formula for solving quadratic equations
- 820 -- Al-Khwarizmi -- Persian mathematician, father of _____, writes the Al-Jabr, later transliterated as _____, which introduces systematic algebraic techniques for solving linear and quadratic equations. Translations of his book on arithmetic will introduce the Hindu-Arabic decimal number system to the Western world in the 12th century.

The term algorithm is also named after him.
- 820 -- Al-Mahani conceived the idea of reducing geometrical problems such as doubling the cube to problems in _____.
- 895 -- Thabit ibn Qurra: the only surviving fragment of his original work contains a chapter on the solution and properties of cubic equations. He also generalized the Pythagorean theorem, and discovered the theorem by which pairs of amicable numbers can be found, .
- ca. 900 -- Abu Kamil of Egypt had begun to understand what we would write in symbols as $x^n \cdot x^m = x^{m+n}$
- 953 -- Al-Karaji is the 'first person to completely free _____ from geometrical operations and to replace them with the arithmetical type of operations which are at the core of _____ today. He was first to define the monomials x, x^2, x^3, … and 1 / x, 1 / x^2, 1 / x^3, … and to give rules for products of any two of these. He started a school of _____ which flourished for several hundreds of years'. He also discovered the binomial theorem for integer exponents, which 'was a major factor in the development of numerical analysis based on the decimal system.'
- 975 -- Al-Batani -- Extended the Indian concepts of sine and cosine to other trigonometrical ratios, like tangent, secant and their inverse functions. Derived the formula: $\sin\alpha = \tan\alpha / \sqrt{1+\tan^2\alpha}$ and $\cos\alpha = 1/\sqrt{1+\tan^2\alpha}$.

- ca. 1000 -- Abū Sahl al-Qūhī (Kuhi) solves equations higher than the second degree.
- ca. 1000 -- Law of sines is discovered by Muslim mathematicians, but it is uncertain who discovers it first between Abu-Mahmud al-Khujandi, Abu Nasr Mansur, and Abu al-Wafa.
- 1070 -- Omar Khayyám begins to write Treatise on Demonstration of Problems of _____ and classifies cubic equations.
- ca. 1100 -- Omar Khayyám 'gave a complete classification of cubic equations with geometric solutions found by means of intersecting conic sections.' He became the first to find general geometric solutions of cubic equations and laid the foundations for the development of analytic geometry and non-Euclidean geometry. He also extracted roots using the decimal system .
- 1100s -- Bhaskara Acharya writes the 'Bijaganita' , which is the first text that recognizes that a positive number has two square roots
- 1130 -- Al-Samawal gave a definition of _____: '[it is concerned] with operating on unknowns using all the arithmetical tools, in the same way as the arithmetician operates on the known.'
- 1135 -- Sharafeddin Tusi followed al-Khayyam's application of _____ to geometry, and wrote a treatise on cubic equations which 'represents an essential contribution to another _____ which aimed to study curves by means of equations, thus inaugurating the beginning of algebraic geometry.'
- ca. 1250 -- Nasir Al-Din Al-Tusi attempts to develop a form of non-Euclidean geometry.
- 1400s -- Nilakantha Somayaji, a Kerala school mathematician, writes the 'Aryabhatiya Bhasya', which contains work on infinite-series expansions, problems of _____, and spherical geometry

- 1520   Scipione dal Ferro develops a method for solving 'depressed' cubic equations (cubic equations without an x^2 term), but does not publish.
- 1535 -- Niccolo Tartaglia independently develops a method for solving depressed cubic equations but also does not publish.
- 1539 -- Gerolamo Cardano learns Tartaglia's method for solving depressed cubics and discovers a method for depressing cubics, thereby creating a method for solving all cubics.
- 1540 -- Lodovico Ferrari solves the quartic equation.

- 1600s - Putumana Somayaji writes the 'Paddhati', which presents a detailed discussion of various trigonometric series
- 1619 - René Descartes discovers analytic geometry (Pierre de Fermat claimed that he also discovered it independently),
- 1619 - Johannes Kepler discovers two of the Kepler-Poinsot polyhedra.
- 1637 - Pierre de Fermat claims to have proven Fermat's Last Theorem in his copy of Diophantus' Arithmetica,
- 1637 - First use of the term imaginary number by René Descartes; it was meant to be derogatory.

- 1722 - Abraham de Moivre states de Moivre's formula connecting trigonometric functions and complex numbers,
- 1733 - Giovanni Gerolamo Saccheri studies what geometry would be like if Euclid's fifth postulate were false,
- 1796 - Carl Friedrich Gauss proves that the regular 17-gon can be constructed using only a compass and straightedge
- 1797 - Caspar Wessel associates vectors with complex numbers and studies complex number operations in geometrical terms,
- 1799 - Carl Friedrich Gauss proves the fundamental theorem of _____,

- 1799 - Paolo Ruffini partially proves the Abel-Ruffini theorem that quintic or higher equations cannot be solved by a general formula,

- 1806 - Louis Poinsot discovers the two remaining Kepler-Poinsot polyhedra.
- 1806 - Jean-Robert Argand publishes proof of the Fundamental theorem of _____ and the Argand diagram,
- 1824 - Niels Henrik Abel partially proves the Abel-Ruffini theorem that the general quintic or higher equations cannot be solved by a general formula involving only arithmetical operations and roots,
- 1829 - Bolyai, Gauss, and Lobachevsky invent hyperbolic non-Euclidean geometry,
- 1832 - Évariste Galois presents a general condition for the solvability of algebraic equations, thereby essentially founding group theory and Galois theory,
- 1837 - Pierre Wantsel proves that doubling the cube and trisecting the angle are impossible with only a compass and straightedge, as well as the full completion of the problem of constructability of regular polygons
- 1843 - William Hamilton discovers the calculus of quaternions and deduces that they are non-commutative,
- 1847 - George Boole formalizes symbolic logic in The Mathematical Analysis of Logic, defining what now is called Boolean _____,
- 1854 - Bernhard Riemann introduces Riemannian geometry,
- 1854 - Arthur Cayley shows that quaternions can be used to represent rotations in four-dimensional space,
- 1858 - August Ferdinand Möbius invents the Möbius strip,
- 1870 - Felix Klein constructs an analytic geometry for Lobachevski's geometry thereby establishing its self-consistency and the logical independence of Euclid's fifth postulate,
- 1873 - Charles Hermite proves that e is transcendental,
- 1878 - Charles Hermite solves the general quintic equation by means of elliptic and modular functions
- 1882 - Ferdinand von Lindemann proves that π is transcendental and that therefore the circle cannot be squared with a compass and straightedge,
- 1882 - Felix Klein invents the Klein bottle,
- 1899 - David Hilbert presents a set of self-consistent geometric axioms in Foundations of Geometry,

- 1901 - Élie Cartan develops the exterior derivative,
- 1905 - Einstein's theory of special relativity.
- 1912 - Luitzen Egbertus Jan Brouwer presents the Brouwer fixed-point theorem,
- 1916 - Einstein's theory of general relativity.
- 1930 - Casimir Kuratowski shows that the three-cottage problem has no solution,
- 1931 - Georges de Rham develops theorems in cohomology and characteristic classes,
- 1933 - Karol Borsuk and Stanislaw Ulam present the Borsuk-Ulam antipodal-point theorem,
- 1955 - H. S. M. Coxeter et al. publish the complete list of uniform polyhedron,
- 1981 - Mikhail Gromov develops the theory of hyperbolic groups, revolutionizing both infinite group theory and global differential geometry,
- 1983 - the classification of finite simple groups, a collaborative work involving some hundred mathematicians and spanning thirty years, is completed,
- 1991 - Alain Connes and John W. Lott develop non-commutative geometry,
- 1998 - Thomas Callister Hales (almost certainly) proves the Kepler conjecture,

- 2003 - Grigori Perelman proves the Poincaré conjecture,
- 2007 - a team of researches throughout North America and Europe used networks of computers to map E8 (mathematics.)

Chapter 2. DEDUCTIVE REASONING

a. ADHM construction
c. ADE classification
b. AA postulate
d. Algebra

5. In geometry, two sets of points are called _____ if one can be transformed into the other by an isometry, i.e., a combination of translations, rotations and reflections. Less formally, two figures are _____ if they have the same shape and size, but are in different positions (for instance one may be rotated, flipped, or simply placed somewhere else).
   a. 1-center problem
   c. Congruent
   b. 11-cell
   d. -module

6. In mathematics, the _____ of a real number is its numerical value without regard to its sign. So, for example, 3 is the _____ of both 3 and −3.

The _____ of a number a is denoted by $|a|$.

   a. AA postulate
   c. ADE classification
   b. ADHM construction
   d. Absolute value

7. In chemistry, the _____ molecular geometry describes the arrangement of three or more atoms placed at an expected bond angle of 180°. _____ organic molecules, e.g. acetylene, are often described by invoking sp orbital hybridization for the carbon centers. Many _____ molecules exist, prominent examples include CO_2, HCN, and xenon difluoride.
   a. -module
   c. 11-cell
   b. 1-center problem
   d. Linear

8. where a is any scalar. A function which satisfies these properties is called a linear function, or more generally a linear map. This property makes _____ s particularly easy to solve and reason about.
   a. -module
   c. 1-center problem
   b. 11-cell
   d. Linear equation

9. In mathematics, a _____ is a convincing demonstration (within the accepted standards of the field) that some mathematical statement is necessarily true. _____ s are obtained from deductive reasoning, rather than from inductive or empirical arguments. That is, a _____ must demonstrate that a statement is true in all cases, without a single exception.
   a. Theorem
   c. Logical axioms
   b. Contrapositive
   d. Proof

10. In logic, _____ is a form of proof that establishes the truth or validity of a proposition by demonstrating the truth or validity of the converse of its negated parts.

In other words, to prove by contraposition that $P \Rightarrow Q$, prove that $\neg Q \Rightarrow \neg P$.

   a. 11-cell
   c. -module
   b. 1-center problem
   d. Proof by contrapositive

11. A _____ is a simple shape of Euclidean geometry consisting of those points in a plane which are the same distance from a given point called the centre. The common distance of the points of a _____ from its center is called its radius.

_____s are simple closed curves which divide the plane into two regions, an interior and an exterior.

a. 11-cell
b. 1-center problem
c. -module
d. Circle

12. In vernacular terms, this states 'If P then Q', or, 'If Socrates is a man then Socrates is human.' In a conditional such as this, P is called the antecedent and Q the consequent. One statement is the _____ of the other just when its antecedent is the negated consequent of the other, and vice-versa. The _____ of the given example statement would be:

$$(\neg Q \to \neg P)$$

That is, 'If not-Q then not-P', or more clearly, 'If Q is not the case, then P is not the case.' Using our example, this is rendered 'If Socrates is not human, then Socrates is not a man.' This statement is said to be contraposed to the original, and is logically equivalent to it.

a. Logical axioms
b. Logically equivalent
c. Theorem
d. Contrapositive

13. The _____ is the middle point of a line segment. It is equidistant from both endpoints. The formula for determining the _____ of a segment in the plane, with endpoints and is

$$\left(\frac{x_1 + x_2}{2}, \frac{y_1 + y_2}{2}\right).$$

In three-dimensional Cartesian space, the _____ formula is

$$\left(\frac{x_1 + x_2}{2}, \frac{y_1 + y_2}{2}, \frac{z_1 + z_2}{2}\right).$$

_____ used in algebra 1=rectangles _____ used in algebra 2=triangles _____ used in geometry=circles

- Astrology _____s
- Median
- Segment bisector
- Numerical Integration

a. Golden angle
c. Quincunx
b. Parallel postulate
d. Midpoint

14. In formal mathematical logic, the concept of a _____ may be taken to mean a formula that can be derived according to the derivation rules of a fixed formal system. The statements of a theory as expressed in a formal language are called its elementary _____s and are said to be true.

The essential property of _____s is that they are derivable using a fixed set of inference rules and axioms without any additional assumptions.

a. Proof
c. Theorem
b. Rule of inference
d. Logical axioms

15. In geometry and trigonometry, an _____ is the figure formed by two rays sharing a common endpoint, called the vertex of the _____ . The magnitude of the _____ is the 'amount of rotation' that separates the two rays, and can be measured by considering the length of circular arc swept out when one ray is rotated about the vertex to coincide with the other Where there is no possibility of confusion, the term '_____' is used interchangeably for both the geometric configuration itself and for its angular magnitude (which is simply a numerical quantity.)

a. ADHM construction
c. AA postulate
b. ADE classification
d. Angle

16. In geometry, bisection is the division of something into two equal or congruent parts, usually by a line, which is then called a bisector. The most often considered types of bisectors are segment bisectors and _____. Bisection of a line segment using a compass and ruler Bisection of an angle using a compass and ruler

a. Inscribed sphere
c. Angle bisectors
b. Axis of symmetry
d. Annulus

17. In geometry, a _____ is any polygon with twelve sides and twelve angles.

It usually refers to a regular _____, having all sides of equal length and all angles equal to 150>°. Its Schl>äfli symbol is {12}.

a. Golygon
c. Dodecagon
b. Hexagon
d. Simple polygon

18. _____, sometimes called deductive logic, is reasoning which constructs or evaluates deductive arguments. In logic, an argument is said to be deductive when the truth of the conclusion is purported to follow necessarily or be a logical consequence of the premises and (consequently) its corresponding conditional is a necessary truth. Deductive arguments are said to be valid or invalid, never true or false.

a. 1-center problem
c. -module
b. 11-cell
d. Deductive reasoning

19. A _____ is one of the basic shapes of geometry: a polygon with three corners or vertices and three sides or edges which are line segments. A _____ with vertices A, B, and C is denoted ABC.

In Euclidean geometry any three non-collinear points determine a unique _____ and a unique plane (i.e. a two-dimensional Euclidean space.)

   a. -module
   b. 1-center problem
   c. Triangle
   d. 11-cell

20. A pair of angles whose sum are 90 degrees are _____.

If the two _____ are adjacent (i.e. have a common vertex and share just one side) their non-shared sides form a right angle.

In Euclidean geometry, the two acute angles in a right triangle are complementary, because the sum of internal angles of a triangle is 180 degrees, and the right angle itself accounts for ninety degrees.

   a. Medial triangle
   b. Concyclic points
   c. Skew lines
   d. Complementary angles

21. A pair of angles is said to be _____ or opposite if the angles share the same vertex and are bounded by the same pair of lines but are opposite to each other. Such angles are congruent and thus have equal measure. If two line segments, EF and GH, intersect at the point P, they form four angles, EPG, GPF, FPH, and HPE.
   a. Conway polyhedron notation
   b. Mirror image
   c. Complementary angles
   d. Vertical

22. In geometry, two lines or planes (or a line and a plane), are considered _____ to each other if they form congruent adjacent angles (an L-shape.) The term may be used as a noun or adjective. Thus, referring to Figure 1, the line AB is the _____ to CD through the point B. Note that by definition, a line is infinitely long, and strictly speaking AB and CD in this example represent line segments of two infinitely long lines.
   a. Heilbronn triangle problem
   b. Point group in two dimensions
   c. Perpendicular
   d. Partial linear space

23. In each statement above, a is not equal to b. These relations are known as strict _____. The notation a < b may also be read as 'a is strictly less than b'.
   a. ADHM construction
   b. ADE classification
   c. AA postulate
   d. Inequalities

Chapter 3. PARALLEL LINES AND PLANES

1. A _____ of a curve is the envelope of a family of congruent circles centered on the curve. It generalises the concept of _____ lines.

It is sometimes called the offset curve but the term 'offset' often refers also to translation.

   a. Trisectrix of Maclaurin   b. Cissoid
   c. Parallel   d. Cassini oval

2. In mathematics, a _____ is a flat surface. _____s can arise as subspaces of some higher dimensional space, as with the walls of a room, or they may enjoy an independent existence in their own right, as in the setting of Euclidean geometry

   a. Parallelogram law   b. Pendent
   c. Simple polytope   d. Plane

3. In geometry and trigonometry, an _____ is the figure formed by two rays sharing a common endpoint, called the vertex of the _____ . The magnitude of the _____ is the 'amount of rotation' that separates the two rays, and can be measured by considering the length of circular arc swept out when one ray is rotated about the vertex to coincide with the other Where there is no possibility of confusion, the term '_____' is used interchangeably for both the geometric configuration itself and for its angular magnitude (which is simply a numerical quantity.)

   a. AA postulate   b. ADE classification
   c. ADHM construction   d. Angle

4. In combinatorial mathematics, given a collection C of sets, a _____ is a set containing exactly one element from each member of the collection: it is a section of the quotient map induced by the collection. If the original sets are not disjoint, there are several different definitions. One variation is that there is a bijection f from the _____ to C such that x is an element of f (x) for each x in the _____.

   a. Transversal   b. No-three-in-line
   c. Geometric combinatorics   d. -module

5. In mathematics, the _____ of a set S consists of all points of S that are intuitively 'not on the edge of S'. A point that is in the _____ of S is an _____ point of S.

The exterior of a set is the _____ of its complement; it consists of the points that are not in the set or its boundary.

The notion of the _____ of a set is a topological concept; it is not defined for all sets, but it is defined for sets that are a subset of a topological space.

   a. Interior   b. ADHM construction
   c. ADE classification   d. AA postulate

6. In geometry, an _____ is an angle formed by two sides of a simple polygon that share an endpoint, namely, the angle on the inner side of the polygon. A simple polygon has exactly one internal angle per vertex.

If every _____ of a polygon is less than 180>°, the polygon is called convex.

Chapter 3. PARALLEL LINES AND PLANES

a. Annulus
c. Apollonius' theorem
b. Angle bisectors
d. Interior Angle

7. In geometry, a _____ is a circular or semicircular tool for measuring an angle or a circle. The units of measurement utilized are usually degrees.

Some _____s are simple half-discs; these have existed since ancient times.

a. 1-center problem
c. -module
b. 11-cell
d. Protractor

8. _____ is the boundless, three-dimensional extent in which objects and events occur and have relative position and direction. Physical _____ is often conceived in three linear dimensions, although modern physicists usually consider it, with time, to be part of the boundless four-dimensional continuum known as spacetime. In mathematics _____s with different numbers of dimensions and with different underlying structures can be examined.

a. Space
c. 1-center problem
b. 11-cell
d. -module

Chapter 3. PARALLEL LINES AND PLANES   17

9. A timeline of _____ and geometry

    - ca. 2000 BC -- Scotland, Carved Stone Balls exhibit a variety of symmetries including all of the symmetries of Platonic solids.
    - 1800 BC -- Moscow Mathematical Papyrus, findings volume of a frustum
    - 1650 BC -- Rhind Mathematical Papyrus, copy of a lost scroll from around 1850 BC, the scribe Ahmes presents one of the first known approximate values of π at 3.16, the first attempt at squaring the circle, earliest known use of a sort of cotangent, and knowledge of solving first order linear equations
    - 1300 BC -- Berlin papyrus (19th dynasty) contains a quadratic equation and its solution.

    - 800 BC -- Baudhayana, author of the Baudhayana Sulba Sutra, a Vedic Sanskrit geometric text, contains quadratic equations, and calculates the square root of 2 correct to five decimal places
    - ca. 600 BC -- the other Vedic 'Sulba Sutras' use Pythagorean triples, contain of a number of geometrical proofs, and approximate π at 3.16
    - 5th century BC -- Hippocrates of Chios utilizes lunes in an attempt to square the circle
    - 5th century BC -- Apastamba, author of the Apastamba Sulba Sutra, another Vedic Sanskrit geometric text, makes an attempt at squaring the circle and also calculates the square root of 2 correct to five decimal places
    - 530 BC -- Pythagoras studies propositional geometry and vibrating lyre strings; his group also discover the irrationality of the square root of two,
    - 370 BC -- Eudoxus states the method of exhaustion for area determination
    - 300 BC -- Euclid in his Elements studies geometry as an axiomatic system, proves the infinitude of prime numbers and presents the Euclidean algorithm; he states the law of reflection in Catoptrics, and he proves the fundamental theorem of arithmetic
    - 260 BC -- Archimedes proved that the value of π lies between 3 + 1/7 and 3 + 10/71 (approx. 3.1408), that the area of a circle was equal to π multiplied by the square of the radius of the circle and that the area enclosed by a parabola and a straight line is 4/3 multiplied by the area of a triangle with equal base and height. He also gave a very accurate estimate of the value of the square root of 3.
    - 225 BC -- Apollonius of Perga writes On Conic Sections and names the ellipse, parabola, and hyperbola,
    - 150 BC -- Jain mathematicians in India write the 'Sthananga Sutra', which contains work on the theory of numbers, arithmetical operations, geometry, operations with fractions, simple equations, cubic equations, quartic equations, and permutations and combinations
    - 140 BC -- Hipparchus develops the bases of trigonometry.

    - 1st century -- Heron of Alexandria, the earliest fleeting reference to square roots of negative numbers.
    - 250 -- Diophantus uses symbols for unknown numbers in terms of syncopated _____, and writes Arithmetica, one of the earliest treatises on _____
    - ca. 340 -- Pappus of Alexandria states his hexagon theorem and his centroid theorem
    - 500 -- Aryabhata writes the 'Aryabhata-Siddhanta', which first introduces the trigonometric functions and methods of calculating their approximate numerical values. It defines the concepts of sine and cosine, and also contains the earliest tables of sine and cosine values
    - 600s -- Bhaskara I gives a rational approximation of the sine function
    - 600s -- Brahmagupta invents the method of solving indeterminate equations of the second degree and is the first to use _____ to solve astronomical problems. He also develops methods for calculations of the motions and places of various planets, their rising and setting, conjunctions, and the calculation of eclipses of the sun and the moon
    - 628 -- Brahmagupta writes the Brahma-sphuta-siddhanta, where zero is clearly explained, and where the modern place-value Indian numeral system is fully developed. It also gives rules for manipulating both negative and positive numbers, methods for computing square roots, methods of solving linear and quadratic equations, and rules for summing series, Brahmagupta's identity, and the Brahmagupta theorem
    - 700s -- Virasena gives explicit rules for the Fibonacci sequence, gives the derivation of the volume of a frustum using an infinite procedure, and also deals with the logarithm to base 2 and knows its laws
    - 700s -- Shridhara gives the rule for finding the volume of a sphere and also the formula for solving quadratic equations
    - 820 -- Al-Khwarizmi -- Persian mathematician, father of _____, writes the Al-Jabr, later transliterated as _____, which introduces systematic algebraic techniques for solving linear and quadratic equations. Translations of his book on arithmetic will introduce the Hindu-Arabic decimal number system to the Western world in the 12th century.

The term algorithm is also named after him.
- 820 -- Al-Mahani conceived the idea of reducing geometrical problems such as doubling the cube to problems in _____.
- 895 -- Thabit ibn Qurra: the only surviving fragment of his original work contains a chapter on the solution and properties of cubic equations. He also generalized the Pythagorean theorem, and discovered the theorem by which pairs of amicable numbers can be found, .
- ca. 900 -- Abu Kamil of Egypt had begun to understand what we would write in symbols as $x^n \cdot x^m = x^{m+n}$
- 953 -- Al-Karaji is the 'first person to completely free _____ from geometrical operations and to replace them with the arithmetical type of operations which are at the core of _____ today. He was first to define the monomials x, x^2, x^3, â€¦ and 1 / x, 1 / x^2, 1 / x^3, â€¦ and to give rules for products of any two of these. He started a school of _____ which flourished for several hundreds of years'. He also discovered the binomial theorem for integer exponents, which 'was a major factor in the development of numerical analysis based on the decimal system.'
- 975 -- Al-Batani -- Extended the Indian concepts of sine and cosine to other trigonometrical ratios, like tangent, secant and their inverse functions. Derived the formula: $\sin \alpha = \tan \alpha / \sqrt{1 + \tan^2 \alpha}$ and $\cos \alpha = 1 / \sqrt{1 + \tan^2 \alpha}$.

- ca. 1000 -- AbÅ« Sahl al-QÅ«hÄ« (Kuhi) solves equations higher than the second degree.
- ca. 1000 -- Law of sines is discovered by Muslim mathematicians, but it is uncertain who discovers it first between Abu-Mahmud al-Khujandi, Abu Nasr Mansur, and Abu al-Wafa.
- 1070 -- Omar Khayyám begins to write Treatise on Demonstration of Problems of _____ and classifies cubic equations.
- ca. 1100 -- Omar Khayyám 'gave a complete classification of cubic equations with geometric solutions found by means of intersecting conic sections.' He became the first to find general geometric solutions of cubic equations and laid the foundations for the development of analytic geometry and non-Euclidean geometry. He also extracted roots using the decimal system .
- 1100s -- Bhaskara Acharya writes the 'Bijaganita' , which is the first text that recognizes that a positive number has two square roots
- 1130 -- Al-Samawal gave a definition of _____: '[it is concerned] with operating on unknowns using all the arithmetical tools, in the same way as the arithmetician operates on the known.'
- 1135 -- Sharafeddin Tusi followed al-Khayyam's application of _____ to geometry, and wrote a treatise on cubic equations which 'represents an essential contribution to another _____ which aimed to study curves by means of equations, thus inaugurating the beginning of algebraic geometry.'
- ca. 1250 -- Nasir Al-Din Al-Tusi attempts to develop a form of non-Euclidean geometry.
- 1400s -- Nilakantha Somayaji, a Kerala school mathematician, writes the 'Aryabhatiya Bhasya', which contains work on infinite-series expansions, problems of _____, and spherical geometry

- 1520 -- Scipione dal Ferro develops a method for solving 'depressed' cubic equations (cubic equations without an x^2 term), but does not publish.
- 1535 -- Niccolo Tartaglia independently develops a method for solving depressed cubic equations but also does not publish.
- 1539 -- Gerolamo Cardano learns Tartaglia's method for solving depressed cubics and discovers a method for depressing cubics, thereby creating a method for solving all cubics.
- 1540 -- Lodovico Ferrari solves the quartic equation.

- 1600s - Putumana Somayaji writes the 'Paddhati', which presents a detailed discussion of various trigonometric series
- 1619 - René Descartes discovers analytic geometry (Pierre de Fermat claimed that he also discovered it independently),
- 1619 - Johannes Kepler discovers two of the Kepler-Poinsot polyhedra.
- 1637 - Pierre de Fermat claims to have proven Fermat's Last Theorem in his copy of Diophantus' Arithmetica,
- 1637 - First use of the term imaginary number by René Descartes; it was meant to be derogatory.

- 1722 - Abraham de Moivre states de Moivre's formula connecting trigonometric functions and complex numbers,
- 1733 - Giovanni Gerolamo Saccheri studies what geometry would be like if Euclid's fifth postulate were false,
- 1796 - Carl Friedrich Gauss proves that the regular 17-gon can be constructed using only a compass and straightedge
- 1797 - Caspar Wessel associates vectors with complex numbers and studies complex number operations in geometrical terms,
- 1799 - Carl Friedrich Gauss proves the fundamental theorem of _____,

- 1799 - Paolo Ruffini partially proves the Abel-Ruffini theorem that quintic or higher equations cannot be solved by a general formula,

- 1806 - Louis Poinsot discovers the two remaining Kepler-Poinsot polyhedra.
- 1806 - Jean-Robert Argand publishes proof of the Fundamental theorem of _____ and the Argand diagram,
- 1824 - Niels Henrik Abel partially proves the Abel-Ruffini theorem that the general quintic or higher equations cannot be solved by a general formula involving only arithmetical operations and roots,
- 1829 - Bolyai, Gauss, and Lobachevsky invent hyperbolic non-Euclidean geometry,
- 1832 - Évariste Galois presents a general condition for the solvability of algebraic equations, thereby essentially founding group theory and Galois theory,
- 1837 - Pierre Wantsel proves that doubling the cube and trisecting the angle are impossible with only a compass and straightedge, as well as the full completion of the problem of constructability of regular polygons
- 1843 - William Hamilton discovers the calculus of quaternions and deduces that they are non-commutative,
- 1847 - George Boole formalizes symbolic logic in The Mathematical Analysis of Logic, defining what now is called Boolean _____,
- 1854 - Bernhard Riemann introduces Riemannian geometry,
- 1854 - Arthur Cayley shows that quaternions can be used to represent rotations in four-dimensional space,
- 1858 - August Ferdinand Möbius invents the Möbius strip,
- 1870 - Felix Klein constructs an analytic geometry for Lobachevski's geometry thereby establishing its self-consistency and the logical independence of Euclid's fifth postulate,
- 1873 - Charles Hermite proves that e is transcendental,
- 1878 - Charles Hermite solves the general quintic equation by means of elliptic and modular functions
- 1882 - Ferdinand von Lindemann proves that π is transcendental and that therefore the circle cannot be squared with a compass and straightedge,
- 1882 - Felix Klein invents the Klein bottle,
- 1899 - David Hilbert presents a set of self-consistent geometric axioms in Foundations of Geometry,

- 1901 - Élie Cartan develops the exterior derivative,
- 1905 - Einstein's theory of special relativity.
- 1912 - Luitzen Egbertus Jan Brouwer presents the Brouwer fixed-point theorem,
- 1916 - Einstein's theory of general relativity.
- 1930 - Casimir Kuratowski shows that the three-cottage problem has no solution,
- 1931 - Georges de Rham develops theorems in cohomology and characteristic classes,
- 1933 - Karol Borsuk and Stanislaw Ulam present the Borsuk-Ulam antipodal-point theorem,
- 1955 - H. S. M. Coxeter et al. publish the complete list of uniform polyhedron,
- 1981 - Mikhail Gromov develops the theory of hyperbolic groups, revolutionizing both infinite group theory and global differential geometry,
- 1983 - the classification of finite simple groups, a collaborative work involving some hundred mathematicians and spanning thirty years, is completed,
- 1991 - Alain Connes and John W. Lott develop non-commutative geometry,
- 1998 - Thomas Callister Hales (almost certainly) proves the Kepler conjecture,

- 2003 - Grigori Perelman proves the Poincaré conjecture,
- 2007 - a team of researches throughout North America and Europe used networks of computers to map E8 (mathematics.)

a. ADE classification
b. AA postulate
c. ADHM construction
d. Algebra

10. In mathematics, a _____ is a convincing demonstration (within the accepted standards of the field) that some mathematical statement is necessarily true. _____s are obtained from deductive reasoning, rather than from inductive or empirical arguments. That is, a _____ must demonstrate that a statement is true in all cases, without a single exception.
   a. Logical axioms
   b. Theorem
   c. Contrapositive
   d. Proof

11. In logic, _____ is a form of proof that establishes the truth or validity of a proposition by demonstrating the truth or validity of the converse of its negated parts.

In other words, to prove by contraposition that $P \Rightarrow Q$, prove that $\neg Q \Rightarrow \neg P$.

   a. 1-center problem
   b. 11-cell
   c. -module
   d. Proof by contrapositive

12. In vernacular terms, this states 'If P then Q', or, 'If Socrates is a man then Socrates is human.' In a conditional such as this, P is called the antecedent and Q the consequent. One statement is the _____ of the other just when its antecedent is the negated consequent of the other, and vice-versa. The _____ of the given example statement would be:

$$(\neg Q \to \neg P)$$

That is, 'If not-Q then not-P', or more clearly, 'If Q is not the case, then P is not the case.' Using our example, this is rendered 'If Socrates is not human, then Socrates is not a man.' This statement is said to be contraposed to the original, and is logically equivalent to it.

   a. Theorem
   b. Contrapositive
   c. Logically equivalent
   d. Logical axioms

13. In geometry, two lines or planes (or a line and a plane), are considered _____ to each other if they form congruent adjacent angles (an L-shape.) The term may be used as a noun or adjective. Thus, referring to Figure 1, the line AB is the _____ to CD through the point B. Note that by definition, a line is infinitely long, and strictly speaking AB and CD in this example represent line segments of two infinitely long lines.
   a. Partial linear space
   b. Heilbronn triangle problem
   c. Perpendicular
   d. Point group in two dimensions

14. A _____ is one of the basic shapes of geometry: a polygon with three corners or vertices and three sides or edges which are line segments. A _____ with vertices A, B, and C is denoted ABC.

In Euclidean geometry any three non-collinear points determine a unique _____ and a unique plane (i.e. a two-dimensional Euclidean space.)

Chapter 3. PARALLEL LINES AND PLANES

a. 11-cell
c. 1-center problem
b. -module
d. Triangle

15. In Euclidean geometry, an _____ is an orthogonal projection. In particular, in 3D it is an affine, parallel projection of an object onto a perpendicular plane.

A simple _____ onto the plane z = 0 can be defined by the following matrix:

$$P = \begin{bmatrix} 1 & 0 & 0 \\ 0 & 1 & 0 \\ 0 & 0 & 0 \end{bmatrix}$$

For each point v = (v_x, v_y, v_z), the transformed point would be

$$Pv = \begin{bmatrix} 1 & 0 & 0 \\ 0 & 1 & 0 \\ 0 & 0 & 0 \end{bmatrix} \begin{bmatrix} v_x \\ v_y \\ v_z \end{bmatrix} = \begin{bmatrix} v_x \\ v_y \\ 0 \end{bmatrix}$$

Often, it is more useful to use homogeneous coordinates, since translation cannot be accomplished with a 3-by-3 matrix.

a. One-dimensional symmetry group
c. Equal incircles theorem
b. Equiangular lines
d. Orthographic Projection

16. A _____ is a triangle in which one angle is a right angle.

The side opposite the right angle is called the hypotenuse (side [BC] in the figure below.) In addition, the sides adjacent to the right angle are called legs or catheti (singular: cathetus.)

a. Stellation
c. Right triangle
b. Polygonal chain
d. Simple polygon

17 In the geometry of curves a _____ is a point of where the first derivative of curvature is zero. This is typically a local maximum or minimum of curvature. Other special cases may occur, for instance when the second derivative is also zero, or when the curvature is constant.
a. Non-Euclidean crystallographic group
c. Coordinate-induced basis
b. Vertex
d. Holomorphic vector bundle

18. In geometry, an _____ polygon is a polygon which has all sides of the same length.

For instance, an _____ triangle is a triangle of equal edge lengths. All _____ triangles are similar to each other, and have 60 degree internal angles.

Chapter 3. PARALLEL LINES AND PLANES

    a. Octagon
    b. Octadecagon
    c. Enneagram
    d. Equilateral

19. In geometry, an _____ is a triangle in which all three sides are equal. In traditional or Euclidean geometry, _____s are also equiangular; that is, all three internal angles are also congruent to each other and are each 60°. They are regular polygons, and can therefore also be referred to as regular triangles.
    a. ADE classification
    b. Orthocenter
    c. AA postulate
    d. Equilateral Triangle

20. In formal mathematical logic, the concept of a _____ may be taken to mean a formula that can be derived according to the derivation rules of a fixed formal system. The statements of a theory as expressed in a formal language are called its elementary _____s and are said to be true.

The essential property of _____s is that they are derivable using a fixed set of inference rules and axioms without any additional assumptions.

    a. Proof
    b. Rule of inference
    c. Theorem
    d. Logical axioms

21. A _____ is a statement which follows readily from a previously proven statement. In mathematics a _____ typically follows a theorem. The use of the term _____, rather than proposition or theorem, is intrinsically subjective.
    a. 1-center problem
    b. -module
    c. Counterexample
    d. Corollary

22. In geometry a _____ is traditionally a plane figure that is bounded by a closed path or circuit, composed of a finite sequence of straight line segments (i.e., by a closed polygonal chain.) These segments are called its edges or sides, and the points where two edges meet are the _____'s vertices or corners. The interior of the _____ is sometimes called its body.
    a. Hexagram
    b. Dodecagon
    c. Right triangle
    d. Polygon

23. The problem of _____ is a classic problem of compass and straightedge constructions of ancient Greek mathematics. Two tools are allowed

1. An un-marked straightedge, and
2. a compass,

Problem: construct an angle one-third a given arbitrary angle.

With such tools, it is generally impossible. This requires taking a cube root, impossible with the given tools.

    a. 1-center problem
    b. -module
    c. 11-cell
    d. Trisecting the angle

Chapter 3. PARALLEL LINES AND PLANES

24. Angle _____: using only a ruler and a compass, construct an angle that is one-third of a given arbitrary angle. With a straightedge and compass, it is in general impossible. For example, the angle of π/3 radians (60°) cannot be trisected, though, say, 2π/5 radians (72°) may be trisected.
    a. Descartes' theorem
    b. Japanese theorem
    c. Constructible number
    d. Trisection

25. In geometry, a _____ is any polygon with ten sides and ten angles, and usually refers to a regular _____, having all sides of equal length and all internal angles equal to 4>π/5 (144>°.) Its Schl>äfli symbol is {10}. The area of a regular _____ of side length a is given by

    >

    A regular _____ is constructible with a compass and straightedge.

    a. Dodecagon
    b. Hendecagon
    c. Net
    d. Decagon

26. In geometry, a _____ is a polygon with six edges and six vertices. A regular _____ has Schl>äfli symbol {6}. The internal angles of a regular _____ are all 120>° and the _____ has 720 degrees T. It has 6 rotational symmetries and 6 reflection symmetries, making up the dihedral group D_6. The longest diagonals of a regular _____, connecting diametrically opposite vertices, are twice its sides in length.

    a. Hexagon
    b. Regular polygon
    c. Right triangle
    d. Hexadecagon

27. In geometry, an _____ is a polygon that has eight sides. A regular _____ is represented by the Schläfli symbol {8}. A regular _____ is constructible with compass and straightedge.
    a. Isothetic polygon
    b. Octadecagon
    c. Enneadecagon
    d. Octagon

28. In geometry, a _____ is any five-sided polygon. A _____ may be simple or self-intersecting. The internal angles in a simple _____ total 540°.
    a. Right triangle
    b. Simple polygon
    c. Five-pointed star
    d. Pentagon

29. In geometry, a _____ is a polygon with four 'sides' or edges and four vertices or corners. Sometimes, the term quadrangle is used, for analogy with triangle, and sometimes tetragon for consistency with pentagon (5-sided), hexagon (6-sided) and so on. The word _____ is made of the words quad and lateral.
    a. -module
    b. 11-cell
    c. 1-center problem
    d. Quadrilateral

30. In geometry, a polygon can be either _____ or concave.

Chapter 3. PARALLEL LINES AND PLANES

A _____ polygon is a simple polygon whose interior is a _____ set. The following properties of a simple polygon are all equivalent to convexity:

- Every internal angle is less than 180 degrees.
- Every line segment between two vertices remains inside or on the boundary of the polygon.

A simple polygon is strictly _____ if every internal angle is strictly less than 180 degrees. Equivalently, a polygon is strictly _____ if every line segment between two nonadjacent vertices of the polygon is strictly interior to the polygon except at its endpoints.

a. Convex combination
b. Separating axis theorem
c. Supporting hyperplane
d. Convex

31. A _____ is a polygon which is equiangular (all angles are equal in measure) and equilateral (all sides have the same length.) _____s may be convex or star.

These properties apply to both convex and a star _____s.

a. Constructible polygon
b. Regular polygon
c. Reuleaux triangle
d. Hendecagon

32. An _____ describes the structure and behaviour of applications used in a business, focused on how they interact with each other and with users. It is focused on the data consumed and produced by applications rather than their internal structure. In application portfolio management, the applications are usually mapped to business functions and to application platform technologies.

a. Applications architecture
b. ADHM construction
c. ADE classification
d. AA postulate

33. In geometry, a _____ is a space filling or close packing of polyhedral or higher-dimensional cells, so that there are no gaps. It is an example of the more general mathematical tiling or tessellation in any number of dimensions.

_____s are usually constructed in ordinary Euclidean ('flat') space.

a. Convex uniform honeycomb
b. Cubic honeycomb
c. Hypercubic honeycomb
d. Honeycomb

34. _____, sometimes called deductive logic, is reasoning which constructs or evaluates deductive arguments. In logic, an argument is said to be deductive when the truth of the conclusion is purported to follow necessarily or be a logical consequence of the premises and (consequently) its corresponding conditional is a necessary truth. Deductive arguments are said to be valid or invalid, never true or false.

a. Deductive reasoning
b. 11-cell
c. -module
d. 1-center problem

Chapter 3. PARALLEL LINES AND PLANES

35. Induction or _____, sometimes called inductive logic, is reasoning which takes us 'beyond the confines of our current evidence or knowledge to conclusions about the unknown.' The premises of an inductive argument indicate some degree of support (inductive probability) for the conclusion but do not entail it; i.e. they do not ensure its truth. Induction is used to ascribe properties or relations to types based on an observation instance (i.e., on a number of observations or experiences); or to formulate laws based on limited observations of recurring phenomenal patterns. Induction is employed, for example, in using specific propositions such as:

   This ice is cold.

   a. Axiom
   c. ADE classification
   b. Inductive reasoning
   d. AA postulate

36. A _____ is a number that determines the location of a point along some line or curve. A list of two, three, or more _____ s can be used to determine the location of a point on a surface, volume, or higher-dimensional domain.

   For example, the longitude is a _____ which determines the position of a point along the Earth's equator, and latitude is another _____ that defines a poisition along a meridian.

   a. 11-cell
   c. Coordinate
   b. 1-center problem
   d. -module

37. In each statement above, a is not equal to b. These relations are known as strict _____. The notation a < b may also be read as 'a is strictly less than b'.
   a. AA postulate
   c. Inequalities
   b. ADHM construction
   d. ADE classification

38. In chemistry, the _____ molecular geometry describes the arrangement of three or more atoms placed at an expected bond angle of 180°. _____ organic molecules, e.g. acetylene, are often described by invoking sp orbital hybridization for the carbon centers. Many _____ molecules exist, prominent examples include CO_2, HCN, and xenon difluoride.
   a. -module
   c. 1-center problem
   b. Linear
   d. 11-cell

39. where a is any scalar. A function which satisfies these properties is called a linear function, or more generally a linear map. This property makes _____ s particularly easy to solve and reason about.
   a. 1-center problem
   c. 11-cell
   b. -module
   d. Linear equation

40. In mathematics, an _____ is a collection of objects having two coordinates (or entries or projections), such that one can always uniquely determine the object, which is the first coordinate (or first entry or left projection) of the pair as well as the second coordinate (or second entry or right projection.) If the first coordinate is a and the second is b, the usual notation for an _____ is (a, b.) The pair is 'ordered' in that (a, b) differs from (b, a) unless a = b.
   a. ADE classification
   c. AA postulate
   b. Ordered pair
   d. ADHM construction

Chapter 3. PARALLEL LINES AND PLANES

41. In mathematics, the _____ of a Euclidean space is a special point, usually denoted by the letter O, used as a fixed point of reference for the geometry of the surrounding space. In a Cartesian coordinate system, the _____ is the point where the axes of the system intersect. In Euclidean geometry, the _____ may be chosen freely as any convenient point of reference.
   a. Origin
   b. Apex
   c. Apollonius' theorem
   d. Adams-hemisphere-in-a-square

42. In mathematics, the _____ of a real number is its numerical value without regard to its sign. So, for example, 3 is the _____ of both 3 and −3.

   The _____ of a number a is denoted by | a | .

   a. AA postulate
   b. ADHM construction
   c. Absolute value
   d. ADE classification

43. _____ is the study of mathematical structures that are fundamentally discrete rather than continuous. Real numbers and rational numbers have the property that between any two numbers a third can be found, and consequently these numbers vary 'smoothly'. The objects generally studied in _____ - such as integers, graphs, and statements in logic - do not vary smoothly in this way, but have distinct, separated values.
   a. -module
   b. 1-center problem
   c. Discrete mathematics
   d. 11-cell

44. In mathematics, a (B, N) _____ is a structure on groups of Lie type that allows one to give uniform proofs of many results, instead of giving a large number of case-by-case proofs. Roughly speaking, it shows that all such groups are similar to the general linear group over a field. They were invented by the mathematician Jacques Tits, and are also sometimes known as Tits systems.
   a. Hanna Neumann conjecture
   b. Dihedral group
   c. Free group
   d. Pair

Chapter 4. CONGRUENT TRIANGLES

1. In geometry and trigonometry, an _____ is the figure formed by two rays sharing a common endpoint, called the vertex of the _____ . The magnitude of the _____ is the 'amount of rotation' that separates the two rays, and can be measured by considering the length of circular arc swept out when one ray is rotated about the vertex to coincide with the other Where there is no possibility of confusion, the term '_____' is used interchangeably for both the geometric configuration itself and for its angular magnitude (which is simply a numerical quantity.)
   a. Angle
   b. ADHM construction
   c. AA postulate
   d. ADE classification

2. In geometry, two sets of points are called _____ if one can be transformed into the other by an isometry, i.e., a combination of translations, rotations and reflections. Less formally, two figures are _____ if they have the same shape and size, but are in different positions (for instance one may be rotated, flipped, or simply placed somewhere else).
   a. 11-cell
   b. Congruent
   c. 1-center problem
   d. -module

3. A _____ is one of the basic shapes of geometry: a polygon with three corners or vertices and three sides or edges which are line segments. A _____ with vertices A, B, and C is denoted ABC.

   In Euclidean geometry any three non-collinear points determine a unique _____ and a unique plane (i.e. a two-dimensional Euclidean space.)

   a. -module
   b. 1-center problem
   c. 11-cell
   d. Triangle

4. In geometry a _____ is traditionally a plane figure that is bounded by a closed path or circuit, composed of a finite sequence of straight line segments (i.e., by a closed polygonal chain.) These segments are called its edges or sides, and the points where two edges meet are the _____'s vertices or corners. The interior of the _____ is sometimes called its body.
   a. Right triangle
   b. Hexagram
   c. Dodecagon
   d. Polygon

5. In mathematics, a _____ is a convincing demonstration (within the accepted standards of the field) that some mathematical statement is necessarily true. _____s are obtained from deductive reasoning, rather than from inductive or empirical arguments. That is, a _____ must demonstrate that a statement is true in all cases, without a single exception.
   a. Logical axioms
   b. Theorem
   c. Proof
   d. Contrapositive

6. A _____ is a building where the outer surfaces are triangular and converge at a point. The base of a _____ is usually trilateral or quadrilateral (but may be of any polygon shape), meaning that a _____ usually has four or five faces. A _____'s design, with the majority of the weight closer to the ground, means that less material higher up on the _____ will be pushing down from above: this allowed early civilizations to create stable monumental structures.
   a. 1-center problem
   b. -module
   c. 11-cell
   d. Pyramid

7. In geometry, two lines or planes (or a line and a plane), are considered _____ to each other if they form congruent adjacent angles (an L-shape.) The term may be used as a noun or adjective. Thus, referring to Figure 1, the line AB is the _____ to CD through the point B. Note that by definition, a line is infinitely long, and strictly speaking AB and CD in this example represent line segments of two infinitely long lines.
   a. Point group in two dimensions
   b. Heilbronn triangle problem
   c. Partial linear space
   d. Perpendicular

8. In mathematics, a _____ is a flat surface. _____s can arise as subspaces of some higher dimensional space, as with the walls of a room, or they may enjoy an independent existence in their own right, as in the setting of Euclidean geometry
   a. Parallelogram law
   b. Pendent
   c. Simple polytope
   d. Plane

9. In logic, _____ is a form of proof that establishes the truth or validity of a proposition by demonstrating the truth or validity of the converse of its negated parts.

In other words, to prove by contraposition that $P \Rightarrow Q$, prove that $\neg Q \Rightarrow \neg P$.

   a. Proof by contrapositive
   b. -module
   c. 11-cell
   d. 1-center problem

10. In vernacular terms, this states 'If P then Q', or, 'If Socrates is a man then Socrates is human.' In a conditional such as this, P is called the antecedent and Q the consequent. One statement is the _____ of the other just when its antecedent is the negated consequent of the other, and vice-versa. The _____ of the given example statement would be:

$$(\neg Q \to \neg P)$$

That is, 'If not-Q then not-P', or more clearly, 'If Q is not the case, then P is not the case.' Using our example, this is rendered 'If Socrates is not human, then Socrates is not a man.' This statement is said to be contraposed to the original, and is logically equivalent to it.

   a. Contrapositive
   b. Logically equivalent
   c. Logical axioms
   d. Theorem

11. An _____ describes the structure and behaviour of applications used in a business, focused on how they interact with each other and with users. It is focused on the data consumed and produced by applications rather than their internal structure. In application portfolio management, the applications are usually mapped to business functions and to application platform technologies.
   a. ADE classification
   b. ADHM construction
   c. AA postulate
   d. Applications architecture

12. In linear algebra, a (linear) _____ is a subset of a vector space that is closed under multiplication by positive scalars. In other words, a subset C of a real vector space V is a _____ if and only if >λx belongs to C for any x in C and any positive scalar >λ of V (or, more succinctly, if and only if >λC = C for any positive scalar >λ.)

Chapter 4. CONGRUENT TRIANGLES

A _____ is said to be pointed if it includes the null vector (origin) 0; otherwise it is said to be blunt.

a. Prismatic surface
b. Centerpoint
c. Complex line
d. Cone

13. In geometry, an _____ polygon is a polygon which has all sides of the same length.

For instance, an _____ triangle is a triangle of equal edge lengths. All _____ triangles are similar to each other, and have 60 degree internal angles.

a. Enneagram
b. Equilateral
c. Octadecagon
d. Octagon

14. In geometry, an _____ is a triangle in which all three sides are equal. In traditional or Euclidean geometry, _____s are also equiangular; that is, all three internal angles are also congruent to each other and are each 60°. They are regular polygons, and can therefore also be referred to as regular triangles.

a. AA postulate
b. Orthocenter
c. ADE classification
d. Equilateral Triangle

15. A _____ is the longest side of a right triangle, the side opposite the right angle. The length of the _____ of a right triangle can be found using the Pythagorean theorem, which states that the square of the length of the _____ equals the sum of the squares of the lengths of the other two sides.

For example, if one of the other sides has a length of 3 meters (when squared, 9 m^2) and the other has a length of 4 m (when squared, 16 m^2.)

a. Hinge theorem
b. Conway polyhedron notation
c. Hypotenuse
d. Confocal

16. A _____ is a triangle in which one angle is a right angle.

The side opposite the right angle is called the hypotenuse (side [BC] in the figure below.) In addition, the sides adjacent to the right angle are called legs or catheti (singular: cathetus.)

a. Right triangle
b. Stellation
c. Simple polygon
d. Polygonal chain

17. In probability theory and statistics, a _____ is described as the number separating the higher half of a sample, a population from the lower half. The _____ of a finite list of numbers can be found by arranging all the observations from lowest value to highest value and picking the middle one. If there is an even number of observations, the _____ is not unique, so one often takes the mean of the two middle values.

a. 11-cell
b. Median
c. -module
d. 1-center problem

18. A _____ is one of the most curvilinear basic geometric shapes:It has two faces, zero vertices, and zero edges. The surface formed by the points at a fixed distance from a given straight line, the axis of the _____. The solid enclosed by this surface and by two planes perpendicular to the axis is also called a _____.
  a. -module
  b. 11-cell
  c. 1-center problem
  d. Cylinder

19. In geometry, a figure with one pair of parallel sides is referred to as _____ in American English, and as a trapezium in British English. A _____ with vertices ABCD is denoted ABCD.

In North America, the term trapezium is used to refer to a quadrilateral with no parallel sides.

  a. Trapezoid
  b. -module
  c. Rhomboid
  d. Tangential quadrilateral

20. In geometry, bisection is the division of something into two equal or congruent parts, usually by a line, which is then called a bisector. The most often considered types of bisectors are segment bisectors and angle bisectors. Bisection of a line segment using a compass and ruler Bisection of an angle using a compass and ruler Line DE bisects line AB at D, line EF is a _____ of segment AD at C and the interior bisector of right angle AED

A line segment bisector passes through the midpoint of the segment.

  a. Perpendicular bisector
  b. 1-center problem
  c. 11-cell
  d. -module

21. In geometry, bisection is the division of something into two equal or congruent parts, usually by a line, which is then called a bisector. The most often considered types of bisectors are segment bisectors and _____. Bisection of a line segment using a compass and ruler Bisection of an angle using a compass and ruler
  a. Axis of symmetry
  b. Annulus
  c. Inscribed sphere
  d. Angle bisectors

22. In geometry, topology and related branches of mathematics a spatial _____ describes a specific object within a given space that consists of neither volume, area, length, nor any other higher dimensional analogue. Thus, a _____ is a 0-dimensional object. Because of their nature as one of the simplest geometric concepts, they are often used in one form or another as the fundamental constituents of geometry, physics, vector graphics, and many other fields.
  a. 11-cell
  b. Point
  c. -module
  d. 1-center problem

Chapter 4. CONGRUENT TRIANGLES

23. A timeline of _____ and geometry

- ca. 2000 BC -- Scotland, Carved Stone Balls exhibit a variety of symmetries including all of the symmetries of Platonic solids.
- 1800 BC -- Moscow Mathematical Papyrus, findings volume of a frustum
- 1650 BC -- Rhind Mathematical Papyrus, copy of a lost scroll from around 1850 BC, the scribe Ahmes presents one of the first known approximate values of π at 3.16, the first attempt at squaring the circle, earliest known use of a sort of cotangent, and knowledge of solving first order linear equations
- 1300 BC -- Berlin papyrus (19th dynasty) contains a quadratic equation and its solution.

- 800 BC -- Baudhayana, author of the Baudhayana Sulba Sutra, a Vedic Sanskrit geometric text, contains quadratic equations, and calculates the square root of 2 correct to five decimal places
- ca. 600 BC -- the other Vedic 'Sulba Sutras' use Pythagorean triples, contain of a number of geometrical proofs, and approximate π at 3.16
- 5th century BC -- Hippocrates of Chios utilizes lunes in an attempt to square the circle
- 5th century BC -- Apastamba, author of the Apastamba Sulba Sutra, another Vedic Sanskrit geometric text, makes an attempt at squaring the circle and also calculates the square root of 2 correct to five decimal places
- 530 BC -- Pythagoras studies propositional geometry and vibrating lyre strings; his group also discover the irrationality of the square root of two,
- 370 BC -- Eudoxus states the method of exhaustion for area determination
- 300 BC -- Euclid in his Elements studies geometry as an axiomatic system, proves the infinitude of prime numbers and presents the Euclidean algorithm; he states the law of reflection in Catoptrics, and he proves the fundamental theorem of arithmetic
- 260 BC -- Archimedes proved that the value of π lies between 3 + 1/7 and 3 + 10/71 (approx. 3.1408), that the area of a circle was equal to π multiplied by the square of the radius of the circle and that the area enclosed by a parabola and a straight line is 4/3 multiplied by the area of a triangle with equal base and height. He also gave a very accurate estimate of the value of the square root of 3.
- 225 BC -- Apollonius of Perga writes On Conic Sections and names the ellipse, parabola, and hyperbola,
- 150 BC -- Jain mathematicians in India write the 'Sthananga Sutra', which contains work on the theory of numbers, arithmetical operations, geometry, operations with fractions, simple equations, cubic equations, quartic equations, and permutations and combinations
- 140 BC -- Hipparchus develops the bases of trigonometry.

- 1st century -- Heron of Alexandria, the earliest fleeting reference to square roots of negative numbers.
- 250 -- Diophantus uses symbols for unknown numbers in terms of syncopated _____, and writes Arithmetica, one of the earliest treatises on _____
- ca. 340 -- Pappus of Alexandria states his hexagon theorem and his centroid theorem
- 500 -- Aryabhata writes the 'Aryabhata-Siddhanta', which first introduces the trigonometric functions and methods of calculating their approximate numerical values. It defines the concepts of sine and cosine, and also contains the earliest tables of sine and cosine values
- 600s -- Bhaskara I gives a rational approximation of the sine function
- 600s -- Brahmagupta invents the method of solving indeterminate equations of the second degree and is the first to use _____ to solve astronomical problems. He also develops methods for calculations of the motions and places of various planets, their rising and setting, conjunctions, and the calculation of eclipses of the sun and the moon
- 628 -- Brahmagupta writes the Brahma-sphuta-siddhanta, where zero is clearly explained, and where the modern place-value Indian numeral system is fully developed. It also gives rules for manipulating both negative and positive numbers, methods for computing square roots, methods of solving linear and quadratic equations, and rules for summing series, Brahmagupta's identity, and the Brahmagupta theorem
- 700s -- Virasena gives explicit rules for the Fibonacci sequence, gives the derivation of the volume of a frustum using an infinite procedure, and also deals with the logarithm to base 2 and knows its laws
- 700s -- Shridhara gives the rule for finding the volume of a sphere and also the formula for solving quadratic equations
- 820 -- Al-Khwarizmi -- Persian mathematician, father of _____, writes the Al-Jabr, later transliterated as _____, which introduces systematic algebraic techniques for solving linear and quadratic equations. Translations of his book on arithmetic will introduce the Hindu-Arabic decimal number system to the Western world in the 12th century.

The term algorithm is also named after him.
- 820 -- Al-Mahani conceived the idea of reducing geometrical problems such as doubling the cube to problems in _____.
- 895 -- Thabit ibn Qurra: the only surviving fragment of his original work contains a chapter on the solution and properties of cubic equations. He also generalized the Pythagorean theorem, and discovered the theorem by which pairs of amicable numbers can be found, .
- ca. 900 -- Abu Kamil of Egypt had begun to understand what we would write in symbols as $x^n \cdot x^m = x^{m+n}$
- 953 -- Al-Karaji is the 'first person to completely free _____ from geometrical operations and to replace them with the arithmetical type of operations which are at the core of _____ today. He was first to define the monomials x, x^2, x^3, … and 1 / x, 1 / x^2, 1 / x^3, … and to give rules for products of any two of these. He started a school of _____ which flourished for several hundreds of years'. He also discovered the binomial theorem for integer exponents, which 'was a major factor in the development of numerical analysis based on the decimal system.'
- 975 -- Al-Batani -- Extended the Indian concepts of sine and cosine to other trigonometrical ratios, like tangent, secant and their inverse functions. Derived the formula: $\sin \alpha = \tan \alpha / \sqrt{1 + \tan^2 \alpha}$ and $\cos \alpha = 1 / \sqrt{1 + \tan^2 \alpha}$.
- ca. 1000 -- Abū Sahl al-Qūhī (Kuhi) solves equations higher than the second degree.
- ca. 1000 -- Law of sines is discovered by Muslim mathematicians, but it is uncertain who discovers it first between Abu-Mahmud al-Khujandi, Abu Nasr Mansur, and Abu al-Wafa.
- 1070 -- Omar Khayyám begins to write Treatise on Demonstration of Problems of _____ and classifies cubic equations.
- ca. 1100 -- Omar Khayyám 'gave a complete classification of cubic equations with geometric solutions found by means of intersecting conic sections.' He became the first to find general geometric solutions of cubic equations and laid the foundations for the development of analytic geometry and non-Euclidean geometry. He also extracted roots using the decimal system .
- 1100s -- Bhaskara Acharya writes the 'Bijaganita' , which is the first text that recognizes that a positive number has two square roots
- 1130 -- Al-Samawal gave a definition of _____: '[it is concerned] with operating on unknowns using all the arithmetical tools, in the same way as the arithmetician operates on the known.'
- 1135 -- Sharafeddin Tusi followed al-Khayyam's application of _____ to geometry, and wrote a treatise on cubic equations which 'represents an essential contribution to another _____ which aimed to study curves by means of equations, thus inaugurating the beginning of algebraic geometry.'
- ca. 1250 -- Nasir Al-Din Al-Tusi attempts to develop a form of non-Euclidean geometry.
- 1400s -- Nilakantha Somayaji, a Kerala school mathematician, writes the 'Aryabhatiya Bhasya', which contains work on infinite-series expansions, problems of _____, and spherical geometry

- 1520 -- Scipione dal Ferro develops a method for solving 'depressed' cubic equations (cubic equations without an x^2 term), but does not publish.
- 1535 -- Niccolo Tartaglia independently develops a method for solving depressed cubic equations but also does not publish.
- 1539 -- Gerolamo Cardano learns Tartaglia's method for solving depressed cubics and discovers a method for depressing cubics, thereby creating a method for solving all cubics.
- 1540 -- Lodovico Ferrari solves the quartic equation.

- 1600s - Putumana Somayaji writes the 'Paddhati', which presents a detailed discussion of various trigonometric series
- 1619 - René Descartes discovers analytic geometry (Pierre de Fermat claimed that he also discovered it independently),
- 1619 - Johannes Kepler discovers two of the Kepler-Poinsot polyhedra.
- 1637 - Pierre de Fermat claims to have proven Fermat's Last Theorem in his copy of Diophantus' Arithmetica,
- 1637 - First use of the term imaginary number by René Descartes; it was meant to be derogative.

- 1722 - Abraham de Moivre states de Moivre's formula connecting trigonometric functions and complex numbers,
- 1733 - Giovanni Gerolamo Saccheri studies what geometry would be like if Euclid's fifth postulate were false,
- 1796 - Carl Friedrich Gauss proves that the regular 17-gon can be constructed using only a compass and straightedge
- 1797 - Caspar Wessel associates vectors with complex numbers and studies complex number operations in geometrical terms,
- 1799 - Carl Friedrich Gauss proves the fundamental theorem of _____,

- 1799 - Paolo Ruffini partially proves the Abel-Ruffini theorem that quintic or higher equations cannot be solved by a general formula,

- 1806 - Louis Poinsot discovers the two remaining Kepler-Poinsot polyhedra.
- 1806 - Jean-Robert Argand publishes proof of the Fundamental theorem of _____ and the Argand diagram,
- 1824 - Niels Henrik Abel partially proves the Abel-Ruffini theorem that the general quintic or higher equations cannot be solved by a general formula involving only arithmetical operations and roots,
- 1829 - Bolyai, Gauss, and Lobachevsky invent hyperbolic non-Euclidean geometry,
- 1832 - Évariste Galois presents a general condition for the solvability of algebraic equations, thereby essentially founding group theory and Galois theory,
- 1837 - Pierre Wantsel proves that doubling the cube and trisecting the angle are impossible with only a compass and straightedge, as well as the full completion of the problem of constructability of regular polygons
- 1843 - William Hamilton discovers the calculus of quaternions and deduces that they are non-commutative,
- 1847 - George Boole formalizes symbolic logic in The Mathematical Analysis of Logic, defining what now is called Boolean _____,
- 1854 - Bernhard Riemann introduces Riemannian geometry,
- 1854 - Arthur Cayley shows that quaternions can be used to represent rotations in four-dimensional space,
- 1858 - August Ferdinand Möbius invents the Möbius strip,
- 1870 - Felix Klein constructs an analytic geometry for Lobachevski's geometry thereby establishing its self-consistency and the logical independence of Euclid's fifth postulate,
- 1873 - Charles Hermite proves that e is transcendental,
- 1878 - Charles Hermite solves the general quintic equation by means of elliptic and modular functions
- 1882 - Ferdinand von Lindemann proves that π is transcendental and that therefore the circle cannot be squared with a compass and straightedge,
- 1882 - Felix Klein invents the Klein bottle,
- 1899 - David Hilbert presents a set of self-consistent geometric axioms in Foundations of Geometry,

- 1901 - Élie Cartan develops the exterior derivative,
- 1905 - Einstein's theory of special relativity.
- 1912 - Luitzen Egbertus Jan Brouwer presents the Brouwer fixed-point theorem,
- 1916 - Einstein's theory of general relativity.
- 1930 - Casimir Kuratowski shows that the three-cottage problem has no solution,
- 1931 - Georges de Rham develops theorems in cohomology and characteristic classes,
- 1933 - Karol Borsuk and Stanislaw Ulam present the Borsuk-Ulam antipodal-point theorem,
- 1955 - H. S. M. Coxeter et al. publish the complete list of uniform polyhedron,
- 1981 - Mikhail Gromov develops the theory of hyperbolic groups, revolutionizing both infinite group theory and global differential geometry,
- 1983 - the classification of finite simple groups, a collaborative work involving some hundred mathematicians and spanning thirty years, is completed,
- 1991 - Alain Connes and John W. Lott develop non-commutative geometry,
- 1998 - Thomas Callister Hales (almost certainly) proves the Kepler conjecture,

- 2003 - Grigori Perelman proves the Poincaré conjecture,
- 2007 - a team of researches throughout North America and Europe used networks of computers to map E8 (mathematics.)

Chapter 4. CONGRUENT TRIANGLES

    a. ADE classification
    b. ADHM construction
    c. AA postulate
    d. Algebra

24. In each statement above, a is not equal to b. These relations are known as strict _____. The notation a < b may also be read as 'a is strictly less than b'.
    a. ADHM construction
    b. Inequalities
    c. AA postulate
    d. ADE classification

25. In chemistry, the _____ molecular geometry describes the arrangement of three or more atoms placed at an expected bond angle of 180°. _____ organic molecules, e.g. acetylene, are often described by invoking sp orbital hybridization for the carbon centers. Many _____ molecules exist, prominent examples include CO_2, HCN, and xenon difluoride.
    a. 1-center problem
    b. -module
    c. 11-cell
    d. Linear

26. where a is any scalar. A function which satisfies these properties is called a linear function, or more generally a linear map. This property makes _____s particularly easy to solve and reason about.
    a. 1-center problem
    b. Linear equation
    c. 11-cell
    d. -module

27. In mathematics, a _____ is a polynomial equation of the second degree. The general form is

$$ax^2 + bx + c = 0$$

The quadratic coefficient a is the coefficient of x^2, the linear coefficient b is the coefficient of x, and c is the constant coefficient, also called the free term or constant term.

_____s are called quadratic because the variable in the leading term is squared.

    a. -module
    b. 11-cell
    c. 1-center problem
    d. Quadratic equation

28. In mathematics, the _____ of a real number is its numerical value without regard to its sign. So, for example, 3 is the _____ of both 3 and −3.

The _____ of a number a is denoted by $|a|$.

    a. ADHM construction
    b. AA postulate
    c. ADE classification
    d. Absolute value

29. A _____ is a simple shape of Euclidean geometry consisting of those points in a plane which are the same distance from a given point called the centre. The common distance of the points of a _____ from its center is called its radius.

_____s are simple closed curves which divide the plane into two regions, an interior and an exterior.

a. -module
b. Circle
c. 11-cell
d. 1-center problem

1. In geometry, a _____ is a quadrilateral with two sets of parallel sides. The opposite or facing sides of a _____ are of equal length, and the opposite angles of a _____ are of equal size. The three-dimensional counterpart of a _____ is a parallelepiped.
   a. -module
   b. Parallelogram
   c. 11-cell
   d. 1-center problem

Chapter 5. QUADRILATERALS 33

2. A timeline of _____ and geometry

- ca. 2000 BC -- Scotland, Carved Stone Balls exhibit a variety of symmetries including all of the symmetries of Platonic solids.
- 1800 BC -- Moscow Mathematical Papyrus, findings volume of a frustum
- 1650 BC -- Rhind Mathematical Papyrus, copy of a lost scroll from around 1850 BC, the scribe Ahmes presents one of the first known approximate values of π at 3.16, the first attempt at squaring the circle, earliest known use of a sort of cotangent, and knowledge of solving first order linear equations
- 1300 BC -- Berlin papyrus (19th dynasty) contains a quadratic equation and its solution.

- 800 BC -- Baudhayana, author of the Baudhayana Sulba Sutra, a Vedic Sanskrit geometric text, contains quadratic equations, and calculates the square root of 2 correct to five decimal places
- ca. 600 BC -- the other Vedic 'Sulba Sutras' use Pythagorean triples, contain of a number of geometrical proofs, and approximate π at 3.16
- 5th century BC -- Hippocrates of Chios utilizes lunes in an attempt to square the circle
- 5th century BC -- Apastamba, author of the Apastamba Sulba Sutra, another Vedic Sanskrit geometric text, makes an attempt at squaring the circle and also calculates the square root of 2 correct to five decimal places
- 530 BC -- Pythagoras studies propositional geometry and vibrating lyre strings; his group also discover the irrationality of the square root of two,
- 370 BC -- Eudoxus states the method of exhaustion for area determination
- 300 BC -- Euclid in his Elements studies geometry as an axiomatic system, proves the infinitude of prime numbers and presents the Euclidean algorithm; he states the law of reflection in Catoptrics, and he proves the fundamental theorem of arithmetic
- 260 BC -- Archimedes proved that the value of π lies between 3 + 1/7 and 3 + 10/71 (approx. 3.1408), that the area of a circle was equal to π multiplied by the square of the radius of the circle and that the area enclosed by a parabola and a straight line is 4/3 multiplied by the area of a triangle with equal base and height. He also gave a very accurate estimate of the value of the square root of 3.
- 225 BC -- Apollonius of Perga writes On Conic Sections and names the ellipse, parabola, and hyperbola,
- 150 BC -- Jain mathematicians in India write the 'Sthananga Sutra', which contains work on the theory of numbers, arithmetical operations, geometry, operations with fractions, simple equations, cubic equations, quartic equations, and permutations and combinations
- 140 BC -- Hipparchus develops the bases of trigonometry.

- 1st century -- Heron of Alexandria, the earliest fleeting reference to square roots of negative numbers.
- 250 -- Diophantus uses symbols for unknown numbers in terms of syncopated _____, and writes Arithmetica, one of the earliest treatises on _____
- ca. 340 -- Pappus of Alexandria states his hexagon theorem and his centroid theorem
- 500 -- Aryabhata writes the 'Aryabhata-Siddhanta', which first introduces the trigonometric functions and methods of calculating their approximate numerical values. It defines the concepts of sine and cosine, and also contains the earliest tables of sine and cosine values
- 600s -- Bhaskara I gives a rational approximation of the sine function
- 600s -- Brahmagupta invents the method of solving indeterminate equations of the second degree and is the first to use _____ to solve astronomical problems. He also develops methods for calculations of the motions and places of various planets, their rising and setting, conjunctions, and the calculation of eclipses of the sun and the moon
- 628 -- Brahmagupta writes the Brahma-sphuta-siddhanta, where zero is clearly explained, and where the modern place-value Indian numeral system is fully developed. It also gives rules for manipulating both negative and positive numbers, methods for computing square roots, methods of solving linear and quadratic equations, and rules for summing series, Brahmagupta's identity, and the Brahmagupta theorem
- 700s -- Virasena gives explicit rules for the Fibonacci sequence, gives the derivation of the volume of a frustum using an infinite procedure, and also deals with the logarithm to base 2 and knows its laws
- 700s -- Shridhara gives the rule for finding the volume of a sphere and also the formula for solving quadratic equations
- 820 -- Al-Khwarizmi -- Persian mathematician, father of _____, writes the Al-Jabr, later transliterated as _____, which introduces systematic algebraic techniques for solving linear and quadratic equations. Translations of his book on arithmetic will introduce the Hindu-Arabic decimal number system to the Western world in the 12th century.

The term algorithm is also named after him.
- 820 -- Al-Mahani conceived the idea of reducing geometrical problems such as doubling the cube to problems in _____.
- 895 -- Thabit ibn Qurra: the only surviving fragment of his original work contains a chapter on the solution and properties of cubic equations. He also generalized the Pythagorean theorem, and discovered the theorem by which pairs of amicable numbers can be found, .
- ca. 900 -- Abu Kamil of Egypt had begun to understand what we would write in symbols as $x^n \cdot x^m = x^{m+n}$
- 953 -- Al-Karaji is the 'first person to completely free _____ from geometrical operations and to replace them with the arithmetical type of operations which are at the core of _____ today. He was first to define the monomials x, x^2, x^3, … and 1 / x, 1 / x^2, 1 / x^3, … and to give rules for products of any two of these. He started a school of _____ which flourished for several hundreds of years'. He also discovered the binomial theorem for integer exponents, which 'was a major factor in the development of numerical analysis based on the decimal system.'
- 975 -- Al-Batani -- Extended the Indian concepts of sine and cosine to other trigonometrical ratios, like tangent, secant and their inverse functions. Derived the formula: $\sin \alpha = \tan \alpha / \sqrt{1 + \tan^2 \alpha}$ and $\cos \alpha = 1 / \sqrt{1 + \tan^2 \alpha}$.
- ca. 1000 -- Abū Sahl al-Qūhī (Kuhi) solves equations higher than the second degree.
- ca. 1000 -- Law of sines is discovered by Muslim mathematicians, but it is uncertain who discovers it first between Abu-Mahmud al-Khujandi, Abu Nasr Mansur, and Abu al-Wafa.
- 1070 -- Omar Khayyám begins to write Treatise on Demonstration of Problems of _____ and classifies cubic equations.
- ca. 1100 -- Omar Khayyám 'gave a complete classification of cubic equations with geometric solutions found by means of intersecting conic sections.' He became the first to find general geometric solutions of cubic equations and laid the foundations for the development of analytic geometry and non-Euclidean geometry. He also extracted roots using the decimal system .
- 1100s -- Bhaskara Acharya writes the 'Bijaganita' , which is the first text that recognizes that a positive number has two square roots
- 1130 -- Al-Samawal gave a definition of _____: '[it is concerned] with operating on unknowns using all the arithmetical tools, in the same way as the arithmetician operates on the known.'
- 1135 -- Sharafeddin Tusi followed al-Khayyam's application of _____ to geometry, and wrote a treatise on cubic equations which 'represents an essential contribution to another _____ which aimed to study curves by means of equations, thus inaugurating the beginning of algebraic geometry.'
- ca. 1250 -- Nasir Al-Din Al-Tusi attempts to develop a form of non-Euclidean geometry.
- 1400s -- Nilakantha Somayaji, a Kerala school mathematician, writes the 'Aryabhatiya Bhasya', which contains work on infinite-series expansions, problems of _____, and spherical geometry

- 1520 -- Scipione dal Ferro develops a method for solving 'depressed' cubic equations (cubic equations without an x^2 term), but does not publish.
- 1535 -- Niccolo Tartaglia independently develops a method for solving depressed cubic equations but also does not publish.
- 1539 -- Gerolamo Cardano learns Tartaglia's method for solving depressed cubics and discovers a method for depressing cubics, thereby creating a method for solving all cubics.
- 1540 -- Lodovico Ferrari solves the quartic equation.

- 1600s - Putumana Somayaji writes the 'Paddhati', which presents a detailed discussion of various trigonometric series
- 1619 - René Descartes discovers analytic geometry (Pierre de Fermat claimed that he also discovered it independently),
- 1619 - Johannes Kepler discovers two of the Kepler-Poinsot polyhedra.
- 1637 - Pierre de Fermat claims to have proven Fermat's Last Theorem in his copy of Diophantus' Arithmetica,
- 1637 - First use of the term imaginary number by René Descartes; it was meant to be derogatory.

- 1722 - Abraham de Moivre states de Moivre's formula connecting trigonometric functions and complex numbers,
- 1733 - Giovanni Gerolamo Saccheri studies what geometry would be like if Euclid's fifth postulate were false,
- 1796 - Carl Friedrich Gauss proves that the regular 17-gon can be constructed using only a compass and straightedge
- 1797 - Caspar Wessel associates vectors with complex numbers and studies complex number operations in geometrical terms,
- 1799 - Carl Friedrich Gauss proves the fundamental theorem of _____,

- 1799 - Paolo Ruffini partially proves the Abel-Ruffini theorem that quintic or higher equations cannot be solved by a general formula,

- 1806 - Louis Poinsot discovers the two remaining Kepler-Poinsot polyhedra.
- 1806 - Jean-Robert Argand publishes proof of the Fundamental theorem of _____ and the Argand diagram,
- 1824 - Niels Henrik Abel partially proves the Abel-Ruffini theorem that the general quintic or higher equations cannot be solved by a general formula involving only arithmetical operations and roots,
- 1829 - Bolyai, Gauss, and Lobachevsky invent hyperbolic non-Euclidean geometry,
- 1832 - Évariste Galois presents a general condition for the solvability of algebraic equations, thereby essentially founding group theory and Galois theory,
- 1837 - Pierre Wantsel proves that doubling the cube and trisecting the angle are impossible with only a compass and straightedge, as well as the full completion of the problem of constructability of regular polygons
- 1843 - William Hamilton discovers the calculus of quaternions and deduces that they are non-commutative,
- 1847 - George Boole formalizes symbolic logic in The Mathematical Analysis of Logic, defining what now is called Boolean _____,
- 1854 - Bernhard Riemann introduces Riemannian geometry,
- 1854 - Arthur Cayley shows that quaternions can be used to represent rotations in four-dimensional space,
- 1858 - August Ferdinand Möbius invents the Möbius strip,
- 1870 - Felix Klein constructs an analytic geometry for Lobachevski's geometry thereby establishing its self-consistency and the logical independence of Euclid's fifth postulate,
- 1873 - Charles Hermite proves that e is transcendental,
- 1878 - Charles Hermite solves the general quintic equation by means of elliptic and modular functions
- 1882 - Ferdinand von Lindemann proves that π is transcendental and that therefore the circle cannot be squared with a compass and straightedge,
- 1882 - Felix Klein invents the Klein bottle,
- 1899 - David Hilbert presents a set of self-consistent geometric axioms in Foundations of Geometry,

- 1901 - Élie Cartan develops the exterior derivative,
- 1905 - Einstein's theory of special relativity.
- 1912 - Luitzen Egbertus Jan Brouwer presents the Brouwer fixed-point theorem,
- 1916 - Einstein's theory of general relativity.
- 1930 - Casimir Kuratowski shows that the three-cottage problem has no solution,
- 1931 - Georges de Rham develops theorems in cohomology and characteristic classes,
- 1933 - Karol Borsuk and Stanislaw Ulam present the Borsuk-Ulam antipodal-point theorem,
- 1955 - H. S. M. Coxeter et al. publish the complete list of uniform polyhedron,
- 1981 - Mikhail Gromov develops the theory of hyperbolic groups, revolutionizing both infinite group theory and global differential geometry,
- 1983 - the classification of finite simple groups, a collaborative work involving some hundred mathematicians and spanning thirty years, is completed,
- 1991 - Alain Connes and John W. Lott develop non-commutative geometry,
- 1998 - Thomas Callister Hales (almost certainly) proves the Kepler conjecture,

- 2003 - Grigori Perelman proves the Poincaré conjecture,
- 2007 - a team of researches throughout North America and Europe used networks of computers to map E8 (mathematics.)

a. ADE classification
b. ADHM construction
c. Algebra
d. AA postulate

3. In mathematics, a _____ is a convincing demonstration (within the accepted standards of the field) that some mathematical statement is necessarily true. _____s are obtained from deductive reasoning, rather than from inductive or empirical arguments. That is, a _____ must demonstrate that a statement is true in all cases, without a single exception.
   a. Logical axioms
   b. Contrapositive
   c. Theorem
   d. Proof

4. In logic, _____ is a form of proof that establishes the truth or validity of a proposition by demonstrating the truth or validity of the converse of its negated parts.

In other words, to prove by contraposition that $P \Rightarrow Q$, prove that $\neg Q \Rightarrow \neg P$.

   a. 1-center problem
   b. -module
   c. 11-cell
   d. Proof by contrapositive

5. In vernacular terms, this states 'If P then Q', or, 'If Socrates is a man then Socrates is human.' In a conditional such as this, P is called the antecedent and Q the consequent. One statement is the _____ of the other just when its antecedent is the negated consequent of the other, and vice-versa. The _____ of the given example statement would be:

$$(\neg Q \rightarrow \neg P)$$

That is, 'If not-Q then not-P', or more clearly, 'If Q is not the case, then P is not the case.' Using our example, this is rendered 'If Socrates is not human, then Socrates is not a man.' This statement is said to be contraposed to the original, and is logically equivalent to it.

   a. Logically equivalent
   b. Contrapositive
   c. Theorem
   d. Logical axioms

6. In geometry, a _____ is a polygon with four 'sides' or edges and four vertices or corners. Sometimes, the term quadrangle is used, for analogy with triangle, and sometimes tetragon for consistency with pentagon (5-sided), hexagon (6-sided) and so on. The word _____ is made of the words quad and lateral.
   a. -module
   b. 11-cell
   c. 1-center problem
   d. Quadrilateral

7. A _____ is one of the basic shapes of geometry: a polygon with three corners or vertices and three sides or edges which are line segments. A _____ with vertices A, B, and C is denoted ABC.

In Euclidean geometry any three non-collinear points determine a unique _____ and a unique plane (i.e. a two-dimensional Euclidean space.)

a. -module
b. 1-center problem
c. 11-cell
d. Triangle

8. A _____ of a curve is the envelope of a family of congruent circles centered on the curve. It generalises the concept of _____ lines.

It is sometimes called the offset curve but the term 'offset' often refers also to translation.

a. Cassini oval
b. Cissoid
c. Trisectrix of Maclaurin
d. Parallel

9. A _____ is an instrument used in geometry, technical drawing and engineering/building to measure distances and/or to rule straight lines. Strictly speaking, the _____ is essentially a straightedge used to rule lines and the calibrated instrument used for determining measurement is called a 'measure'. However, common usage is that a _____ is a calibrated straightedge that can be used for making measurements.

a. -module
b. Ruler
c. 11-cell
d. 1-center problem

10. The _____ is the middle point of a line segment. It is equidistant from both endpoints. The formula for determining the _____ of a segment in the plane, with endpoints and is

$$\left(\frac{x_1 + x_2}{2}, \frac{y_1 + y_2}{2}\right).$$

In three-dimensional Cartesian space, the _____ formula is

$$\left(\frac{x_1 + x_2}{2}, \frac{y_1 + y_2}{2}, \frac{z_1 + z_2}{2}\right).$$

_____ used in algebra 1=rectangles _____ used in algebra 2=triangles _____ used in geometry=circles

- Astrology _____ s
- Median
- Segment bisector
- Numerical Integration

a. Parallel postulate
b. Golden angle
c. Quincunx
d. Midpoint

11. In Euclidean geometry, a _____ is a quadrilateral with four right angles. Equivalently, it is an equiangular quadrilateral, but it is not necessarily equilateral.

A _____ with vertices ABCD would be denoted as ABCD.

- All angles are 90 degrees.
- Opposite sides are equal in length.
- Opposite sides are parallel.
- Diagonals are equal in length and bisect each other.

The formula for the perimeter of a _____.

If a _____ has length l and width w

- it has area A = lw
- perimeter P = 2l + 2w = 2(l + w)
- and each diagonal has length $\sqrt{l^2 + w^2}$.

When the length is equal to the width, the _____ is a square.

a. -module
c. 11-cell
b. Rectangle
d. 1-center problem

12.

Every _____ has two diagonals connecting opposite pairs of vertices. Using congruent triangles, one can prove that the _____ is symmetric across each of these diagonals. It follows that any _____ has the following two properties:

1. Opposite angles of a _____ have equal measure.
2. The two diagonals of a _____ are perpendicular.

a. -module
c. 11-cell
b. 1-center problem
d. Rhombus

13. In Euclidean geometry, a _____ is a regular quadrilateral. This means that it has four equal sides and four equal angles (90 degree angles, or right angles.) A _____ with vertices ABCD would be denoted ABCD.

a. 11-cell
c. 1-center problem
b. Square
d. -module

14. A _____ is a triangle in which one angle is a right angle.

The side opposite the right angle is called the hypotenuse (side [BC] in the figure below.) In addition, the sides adjacent to the right angle are called legs or catheti (singular: cathetus.)

Chapter 5. QUADRILATERALS

a. Stellation
c. Polygonal chain
b. Simple polygon
d. Right triangle

15. In formal mathematical logic, the concept of a _____ may be taken to mean a formula that can be derived according to the derivation rules of a fixed formal system. The statements of a theory as expressed in a formal language are called its elementary _____s and are said to be true.

The essential property of _____s is that they are derivable using a fixed set of inference rules and axioms without any additional assumptions.

a. Logical axioms
c. Theorem
b. Rule of inference
d. Proof

16. In geometry, a figure with one pair of parallel sides is referred to as _____ in American English, and as a trapezium in British English. A _____ with vertices ABCD is denoted ABCD.

In North America, the term trapezium is used to refer to a quadrilateral with no parallel sides.

a. Tangential quadrilateral
c. Rhomboid
b. -module
d. Trapezoid

17. In linear algebra, a (linear) _____ is a subset of a vector space that is closed under multiplication by positive scalars. In other words, a subset C of a real vector space V is a _____ if and only if >λx belongs to C for any x in C and any positive scalar >λ of V (or, more succintly, if and only if >λC = C for any positive scalar >λ.)

A _____ is said to be pointed if it includes the null vector (origin) 0; otherwise it is said to be blunt.

a. Complex line
c. Prismatic surface
b. Centerpoint
d. Cone

18. An _____ is a quadrilateral with a line of symmetry bisecting one pair of opposite sides, making it automatically a trapezoid. Two opposite sides are parallel, the two other sides (legs) are of equal length. The diagonals are of equal length.
a. ADE classification
c. Isosceles Trapezoid
b. AA postulate
d. ADHM construction

19. In probability theory and statistics, a _____ is described as the number separating the higher half of a sample, a population from the lower half. The _____ of a finite list of numbers can be found by arranging all the observations from lowest value to highest value and picking the middle one. If there is an even number of observations, the _____ is not unique, so one often takes the mean of the two middle values.
a. 1-center problem
c. 11-cell
b. -module
d. Median

20. In geometry a _____ is a quadrilateral with two disjoint pairs of congruent adjacent sides, in contrast to a parallelogram, where the congruent sides are opposite. The geometric object is named for the wind-blown, flying _____ , which in its simple form often has this shape.

Equivalently, a _____ is a quadrilateral with an axis of symmetry along one of its diagonals.

a. 1-center problem
b. -module
c. 11-cell
d. Kite

Chapter 6. INEQUALITIES IN GEOMETRY

1. A timeline of _____ and geometry

   - ca. 2000 BC -- Scotland, Carved Stone Balls exhibit a variety of symmetries including all of the symmetries of Platonic solids.
   - 1800 BC -- Moscow Mathematical Papyrus, findings volume of a frustum
   - 1650 BC -- Rhind Mathematical Papyrus, copy of a lost scroll from around 1850 BC, the scribe Ahmes presents one of the first known approximate values of π at 3.16, the first attempt at squaring the circle, earliest known use of a sort of cotangent, and knowledge of solving first order linear equations
   - 1300 BC -- Berlin papyrus (19th dynasty) contains a quadratic equation and its solution.

   - 800 BC -- Baudhayana, author of the Baudhayana Sulba Sutra, a Vedic Sanskrit geometric text, contains quadratic equations, and calculates the square root of 2 correct to five decimal places
   - ca. 600 BC -- the other Vedic 'Sulba Sutras' use Pythagorean triples, contain of a number of geometrical proofs, and approximate π at 3.16
   - 5th century BC -- Hippocrates of Chios utilizes lunes in an attempt to square the circle
   - 5th century BC -- Apastamba, author of the Apastamba Sulba Sutra, another Vedic Sanskrit geometric text, makes an attempt at squaring the circle and also calculates the square root of 2 correct to five decimal places
   - 530 BC -- Pythagoras studies propositional geometry and vibrating lyre strings; his group also discover the irrationality of the square root of two,
   - 370 BC -- Eudoxus states the method of exhaustion for area determination
   - 300 BC -- Euclid in his Elements studies geometry as an axiomatic system, proves the infinitude of prime numbers and presents the Euclidean algorithm; he states the law of reflection in Catoptrics, and he proves the fundamental theorem of arithmetic
   - 260 BC -- Archimedes proved that the value of π lies between 3 + 1/7 and 3 + 10/71 (approx. 3.1408), that the area of a circle was equal to π multiplied by the square of the radius of the circle and that the area enclosed by a parabola and a straight line is 4/3 multiplied by the area of a triangle with equal base and height. He also gave a very accurate estimate of the value of the square root of 3.
   - 225 BC -- Apollonius of Perga writes On Conic Sections and names the ellipse, parabola, and hyperbola,
   - 150 BC -- Jain mathematicians in India write the 'Sthananga Sutra', which contains work on the theory of numbers, arithmetical operations, geometry, operations with fractions, simple equations, cubic equations, quartic equations, and permutations and combinations
   - 140 BC -- Hipparchus develops the bases of trigonometry.

   - 1st century -- Heron of Alexandria, the earliest fleeting reference to square roots of negative numbers.
   - 250 -- Diophantus uses symbols for unknown numbers in terms of syncopated _____, and writes Arithmetica, one of the earliest treatises on _____
   - ca. 340 -- Pappus of Alexandria states his hexagon theorem and his centroid theorem
   - 500 -- Aryabhata writes the 'Aryabhata-Siddhanta', which first introduces the trigonometric functions and methods of calculating their approximate numerical values. It defines the concepts of sine and cosine, and also contains the earliest tables of sine and cosine values
   - 600s -- Bhaskara I gives a rational approximation of the sine function
   - 600s -- Brahmagupta invents the method of solving indeterminate equations of the second degree and is the first to use _____ to solve astronomical problems. He also develops methods for calculations of the motions and places of various planets, their rising and setting, conjunctions, and the calculation of eclipses of the sun and the moon
   - 628 -- Brahmagupta writes the Brahma-sphuta-siddhanta, where zero is clearly explained, and where the modern place-value Indian numeral system is fully developed. It also gives rules for manipulating both negative and positive numbers, methods for computing square roots, methods of solving linear and quadratic equations, and rules for summing series, Brahmagupta's identity, and the Brahmagupta theorem
   - 700s -- Virasena gives explicit rules for the Fibonacci sequence, gives the derivation of the volume of a frustum using an infinite procedure, and also deals with the logarithm to base 2 and knows its laws
   - 700s -- Shridhara gives the rule for finding the volume of a sphere and also the formula for solving quadratic equations
   - 820 -- Al-Khwarizmi -- Persian mathematician, father of _____, writes the Al-Jabr, later transliterated as _____, which introduces systematic algebraic techniques for solving linear and quadratic equations. Translations of his book on arithmetic will introduce the Hindu-Arabic decimal number system to the Western world in the 12th century.

The term algorithm is also named after him.
- 820 -- Al-Mahani conceived the idea of reducing geometrical problems such as doubling the cube to problems in _____.
- 895 -- Thabit ibn Qurra: the only surviving fragment of his original work contains a chapter on the solution and properties of cubic equations. He also generalized the Pythagorean theorem, and discovered the theorem by which pairs of amicable numbers can be found, .
- ca. 900 -- Abu Kamil of Egypt had begun to understand what we would write in symbols as $x^n \cdot x^m = x^{m+n}$
- 953 -- Al-Karaji is the 'first person to completely free _____ from geometrical operations and to replace them with the arithmetical type of operations which are at the core of _____ today. He was first to define the monomials x, x^2, x^3, â€¦ and 1 / x, 1 / x^2, 1 / x^3, â€¦ and to give rules for products of any two of these. He started a school of _____ which flourished for several hundreds of years'. He also discovered the binomial theorem for integer exponents, which 'was a major factor in the development of numerical analysis based on the decimal system.'
- 975 -- Al-Batani -- Extended the Indian concepts of sine and cosine to other trigonometrical ratios, like tangent, secant and their inverse functions. Derived the formula: $\sin \alpha = \tan \alpha / \sqrt{1 + \tan^2 \alpha}$ and $\cos \alpha = 1 / \sqrt{1 + \tan^2 \alpha}$.

- ca. 1000 -- AbÅ« Sahl al-QÅ«hÄ« (Kuhi) solves equations higher than the second degree.
- ca. 1000 -- Law of sines is discovered by Muslim mathematicians, but it is uncertain who discovers it first between Abu-Mahmud al-Khujandi, Abu Nasr Mansur, and Abu al-Wafa.
- 1070 -- Omar Khayyám begins to write Treatise on Demonstration of Problems of _____ and classifies cubic equations.
- ca. 1100 -- Omar Khayyám 'gave a complete classification of cubic equations with geometric solutions found by means of intersecting conic sections.' He became the first to find general geometric solutions of cubic equations and laid the foundations for the development of analytic geometry and non-Euclidean geometry. He also extracted roots using the decimal system .
- 1100s -- Bhaskara Acharya writes the 'Bijaganita' , which is the first text that recognizes that a positive number has two square roots
- 1130 -- Al-Samawal gave a definition of _____: '[it is concerned] with operating on unknowns using all the arithmetical tools, in the same way as the arithmetician operates on the known.'
- 1135 -- Sharafeddin Tusi followed al-Khayyam's application of _____ to geometry, and wrote a treatise on cubic equations which 'represents an essential contribution to another _____ which aimed to study curves by means of equations, thus inaugurating the beginning of algebraic geometry.'
- ca. 1250 -- Nasir Al-Din Al-Tusi attempts to develop a form of non-Euclidean geometry.
- 1400s -- Nilakantha Somayaji, a Kerala school mathematician, writes the 'Aryabhatiya Bhasya', which contains work on infinite-series expansions, problems of _____, and spherical geometry

- 1520 -- Scipione dal Ferro develops a method for solving 'depressed' cubic equations (cubic equations without an x^2 term), but does not publish.
- 1535 -- Niccolo Tartaglia independently develops a method for solving depressed cubic equations but also does not publish.
- 1539 -- Gerolamo Cardano learns Tartaglia's method for solving depressed cubics and discovers a method for depressing cubics, thereby creating a method for solving all cubics.
- 1540 -- Lodovico Ferrari solves the quartic equation.

- 1600s - Putumana Somayaji writes the 'Paddhati', which presents a detailed discussion of various trigonometric series
- 1619 - René Descartes discovers analytic geometry (Pierre de Fermat claimed that he also discovered it independently),
- 1619 - Johannes Kepler discovers two of the Kepler-Poinsot polyhedra.
- 1637 - Pierre de Fermat claims to have proven Fermat's Last Theorem in his copy of Diophantus' Arithmetica,
- 1637 - First use of the term imaginary number by René Descartes; it was meant to be derogatory.

- 1722 - Abraham de Moivre states de Moivre's formula connecting trigonometric functions and complex numbers,
- 1733 - Giovanni Gerolamo Saccheri studies what geometry would be like if Euclid's fifth postulate were false,
- 1796 - Carl Friedrich Gauss proves that the regular 17-gon can be constructed using only a compass and straightedge
- 1797 - Caspar Wessel associates vectors with complex numbers and studies complex number operations in geometrical terms,
- 1799 - Carl Friedrich Gauss proves the fundamental theorem of _____,

- 1799 - Paolo Ruffini partially proves the Abel-Ruffini theorem that quintic or higher equations cannot be solved by a general formula,

- 1806 - Louis Poinsot discovers the two remaining Kepler-Poinsot polyhedra.
- 1806 - Jean-Robert Argand publishes proof of the Fundamental theorem of _____ and the Argand diagram,
- 1824 - Niels Henrik Abel partially proves the Abel-Ruffini theorem that the general quintic or higher equations cannot be solved by a general formula involving only arithmetical operations and roots,
- 1829 - Bolyai, Gauss, and Lobachevsky invent hyperbolic non-Euclidean geometry,
- 1832 - Évariste Galois presents a general condition for the solvability of algebraic equations, thereby essentially founding group theory and Galois theory,
- 1837 - Pierre Wantsel proves that doubling the cube and trisecting the angle are impossible with only a compass and straightedge, as well as the full completion of the problem of constructability of regular polygons
- 1843 - William Hamilton discovers the calculus of quaternions and deduces that they are non-commutative,
- 1847 - George Boole formalizes symbolic logic in The Mathematical Analysis of Logic, defining what now is called Boolean _____,
- 1854 - Bernhard Riemann introduces Riemannian geometry,
- 1854 - Arthur Cayley shows that quaternions can be used to represent rotations in four-dimensional space,
- 1858 - August Ferdinand Möbius invents the Möbius strip,
- 1870 - Felix Klein constructs an analytic geometry for Lobachevski's geometry thereby establishing its self-consistency and the logical independence of Euclid's fifth postulate,
- 1873 - Charles Hermite proves that e is transcendental,
- 1878 - Charles Hermite solves the general quintic equation by means of elliptic and modular functions
- 1882 - Ferdinand von Lindemann proves that π is transcendental and that therefore the circle cannot be squared with a compass and straightedge,
- 1882 - Felix Klein invents the Klein bottle,
- 1899 - David Hilbert presents a set of self-consistent geometric axioms in Foundations of Geometry,

- 1901 - Élie Cartan develops the exterior derivative,
- 1905 - Einstein's theory of special relativity.
- 1912 - Luitzen Egbertus Jan Brouwer presents the Brouwer fixed-point theorem,
- 1916 - Einstein's theory of general relativity.
- 1930 - Casimir Kuratowski shows that the three-cottage problem has no solution,
- 1931 - Georges de Rham develops theorems in cohomology and characteristic classes,
- 1933 - Karol Borsuk and Stanislaw Ulam present the Borsuk-Ulam antipodal-point theorem,
- 1955 - H. S. M. Coxeter et al. publish the complete list of uniform polyhedron,
- 1981 - Mikhail Gromov develops the theory of hyperbolic groups, revolutionizing both infinite group theory and global differential geometry,
- 1983 - the classification of finite simple groups, a collaborative work involving some hundred mathematicians and spanning thirty years, is completed,
- 1991 - Alain Connes and John W. Lott develop non-commutative geometry,
- 1998 - Thomas Callister Hales (almost certainly) proves the Kepler conjecture,

- 2003 - Grigori Perelman proves the Poincaré conjecture,
- 2007 - a team of researches throughout North America and Europe used networks of computers to map E8 (mathematics.)

a. ADE classification
b. ADHM construction
c. Algebra
d. AA postulate

2. In mathematics, an _____ is a statement about the relative size or order of two objects, or about whether they are the same or not

- The notation a < b means that a is less than b.
- The notation a > b means that a is greater than b.
- The notation a ≠ b means that a is not equal to b, but does not say that one is bigger than the other or even that they can be compared in size.

In all these cases, a is not equal to b, hence, '_____'.

These relations are known as strict _____

- The notation a ≤ b means that a is less than or equal to b (or, equivalently, not greater than b);
- The notation a ≥ b means that a is greater than or equal to b (or, equivalently, not smaller than b);

An additional use of the notation is to show that one quantity is much greater than another, normally by several orders of magnitude.

- The notation a .

a. AA postulate
b. ADE classification
c. ADHM construction
d. Inequality

3. In mathematics, the _____ of a real number is its numerical value without regard to its sign. So, for example, 3 is the _____ of both 3 and −3.

The _____ of a number a is denoted by $|a|$.

a. ADHM construction
b. ADE classification
c. AA postulate
d. Absolute value

4. In each statement above, a is not equal to b. These relations are known as strict _____. The notation a < b may also be read as 'a is strictly less than b'.

a. Inequalities
b. AA postulate
c. ADE classification
d. ADHM construction

5. In geometry and trigonometry, an _____ is the figure formed by two rays sharing a common endpoint, called the vertex of the _____ . The magnitude of the _____ is the 'amount of rotation' that separates the two rays, and can be measured by considering the length of circular arc swept out when one ray is rotated about the vertex to coincide with the other Where there is no possibility of confusion, the term '_____' is used interchangeably for both the geometric configuration itself and for its angular magnitude (which is simply a numerical quantity.)

Chapter 6. INEQUALITIES IN GEOMETRY

a. Angle
b. ADHM construction
c. AA postulate
d. ADE classification

6. A _____ is one of the basic shapes of geometry: a polygon with three corners or vertices and three sides or edges which are line segments. A _____ with vertices A, B, and C is denoted ABC.

In Euclidean geometry any three non-collinear points determine a unique _____ and a unique plane (i.e. a two-dimensional Euclidean space.)

a. -module
b. 1-center problem
c. 11-cell
d. Triangle

7. In geometry a _____ is traditionally a plane figure that is bounded by a closed path or circuit, composed of a finite sequence of straight line segments (i.e., by a closed polygonal chain.) These segments are called its edges or sides, and the points where two edges meet are the _____'s vertices or corners. The interior of the _____ is sometimes called its body.

a. Right triangle
b. Hexagram
c. Dodecagon
d. Polygon

8. In vernacular terms, this states 'If P then Q', or, 'If Socrates is a man then Socrates is human.' In a conditional such as this, P is called the antecedent and Q the consequent. One statement is the _____ of the other just when its antecedent is the negated consequent of the other, and vice-versa. The _____ of the given example statement would be:

$$(\neg Q \to \neg P)$$

That is, 'If not-Q then not-P', or more clearly, 'If Q is not the case, then P is not the case.' Using our example, this is rendered 'If Socrates is not human, then Socrates is not a man.' This statement is said to be contraposed to the original, and is logically equivalent to it.

a. Contrapositive
b. Theorem
c. Logically equivalent
d. Logical axioms

9. In computer science, _____s, conditional expressions and conditional constructs are features of a programming language which perform different computations or actions depending on whether a programmer-specified condition evaluates to true or false Apart from the case of branch predication, this is always achieved by selectively altering the control flow based on some condition.

In imperative programming languages, the term '_____' is usually used, whereas in functional programming, the terms 'conditional expression' or 'conditional construct' are preferred, because these terms all have distinct meanings.

a. -module
b. 1-center problem
c. 11-cell
d. Conditional statement

Chapter 6. INEQUALITIES IN GEOMETRY

10. _____s or set diagrams are diagrams that show all hypothetically possible logical relations between a finite collection of sets (groups of things.) _____s were conceived around 1880 by John Venn. They are used in many fields, including set theory, probability, logic, statistics, and computer science.
    a. 11-cell
    b. 1-center problem
    c. -module
    d. Venn diagram

11. In logic and mathematics, logical _____ is a logical operator connecting two statements to assert, p if and only if q where p is a hypothesis and q is a conclusion The operator is denoted using a doubleheaded arrow '↔', an equality sign '=', an equivalence sign '≡', or EQV. It is logically equivalent to ∧, or the XNOR boolean operator.
    a. Theorem
    b. Rule of inference
    c. Logical axioms
    d. Biconditional

12. In logic, statements p and q are _____ if they have the same logical content.

Syntactically, p and q are equivalent if each can be proved from the other. Semantically, p and q are equivalent if they have the same truth value in every model.

    a. Rule of inference
    b. Logically equivalent
    c. Contrapositive
    d. Theorem

13. In mathematics, a _____ is a convincing demonstration (within the accepted standards of the field) that some mathematical statement is necessarily true. _____s are obtained from deductive reasoning, rather than from inductive or empirical arguments. That is, a _____ must demonstrate that a statement is true in all cases, without a single exception.
    a. Logical axioms
    b. Theorem
    c. Contrapositive
    d. Proof

14. In logic, _____ is a form of proof that establishes the truth or validity of a proposition by demonstrating the truth or validity of the converse of its negated parts.

In other words, to prove by contraposition that $P \Rightarrow Q$, prove that $\neg Q \Rightarrow \neg P$.

    a. 1-center problem
    b. Proof by contrapositive
    c. -module
    d. 11-cell

15. In mathematics, the _____ states that for any triangle, the length of a given side must be less than the sum of the other two sides but greater than the difference between the two sides.

In Euclidean geometry and some other geometries this is a theorem. In the Euclidean case, in both the less than or equal to and greater than or equal to statements, equality occurs only if the triangle has a 180>° angle and two 0>° angles, as shown in the bottom example in the image to the right.

    a. 1-center problem
    b. -module
    c. Triangle Inequality
    d. 11-cell

Chapter 6. INEQUALITIES IN GEOMETRY

16. In mathematics, a _____ is a map that transforms an object into its mirror image. For example, a _____ of the small English letter p in respect to a vertical line would look like q. In order to reflect a planar figure one needs the 'mirror' to be a line , while for _____s in the three-dimensional space one would use a plane for a mirror.
    a. Rotation of axes
    b. Point reflection
    c. Translation
    d. Reflection

17. In mathematics, _____ geometry describes hyperbolic and elliptic geometry, which are contrasted with Euclidean geometry. The essential difference between Euclidean and _____ geometry is the nature of parallel lines. Euclid's fifth postulate, the parallel postulate, is equivalent to Playfair's postulate, which states that, within a two-dimensional plane, for any given line l and a point A, which is not on l, there is exactly one line through A that does not intersect l.
    a. Codimension
    b. Coplanar
    c. Coaxial
    d. Non-Euclidean

18. In mathematics, _____ describes hyperbolic and elliptic geometry, which are contrasted with Euclidean geometry. The essential difference between Euclidean and _____ is the nature of parallel lines. Euclid's fifth postulate, the parallel postulate, is equivalent to Playfair's postulate, which states that, within a two-dimensional plane, for any given line l and a point A, which is not on l, there is exactly one line through A that does not intersect l.
    a. Non-Euclidean Geometry
    b. Coxeter group
    c. Linearly separable
    d. Duoprism

19. A _____ of a curve is the envelope of a family of congruent circles centered on the curve. It generalises the concept of _____ lines.

It is sometimes called the offset curve but the term 'offset' often refers also to translation.

    a. Trisectrix of Maclaurin
    b. Parallel
    c. Cissoid
    d. Cassini oval

20. In geometry, the _____ is a distinctive axiom in what is now called Euclidean geometry. It states that:

If a line segment intersects two straight lines forming two interior angles on the same side that sum to less than two right angles, then the two lines, if extended indefinitely, meet on that side on which the angles sum to less than two right angles.

Euclidean geometry is the study of geometry that satisfies all of Euclid's axioms, including the _____.

    a. Hypotenuse
    b. Confocal
    c. Parallel Postulate
    d. Concyclic points

21. A _____ of a sphere is a circle that runs along the surface of that sphere so as to cut it into two equal halves. The _____ therefore has both the same circumference and the same center as the sphere. It is the largest circle that can be drawn on a given sphere.
    a. Line segment
    b. Complementary angles
    c. Great circle
    d. Conway polyhedron notation

Chapter 6. INEQUALITIES IN GEOMETRY

22. In every _____ there is a cuboid with all vertices tangent to the surface of said _____. It immediately becomes apparent that the cuboid inscribed in the _____ must be a cube with all vertices tangent to the surface of the _____.

Formula 1, shown below, finds the length of one side of the inscribed cube, and Formula 2 finds the volume of the inscribed cube.

a. Cone
b. Circumference
c. Sphere
d. Point group in two dimensions

23. A _____ is a simple shape of Euclidean geometry consisting of those points in a plane which are the same distance from a given point called the centre. The common distance of the points of a _____ from its center is called its radius.

_____s are simple closed curves which divide the plane into two regions, an interior and an exterior.

a. 1-center problem
b. Circle
c. -module
d. 11-cell

24. A _____ is a number that determines the location of a point along some line or curve. A list of two, three, or more _____s can be used to determine the location of a point on a surface, volume, or higher-dimensional domain.

For example, the longitude is a _____ which determines the position of a point along the Earth's equator, and latitude is another _____ that defines a poisition along a meridian.

a. 1-center problem
b. -module
c. 11-cell
d. Coordinate

25. In mathematics, an _____ is the finite or bounded case of a conic section, the geometric shape that results from cutting a circular conical or cylindrical surface with an oblique plane . It is also the locus of all points of the plane whose distances to two fixed points add to the same constant.

_____s also arise as images of a circle or a sphere under parallel projection, and some cases of perspective projection.

a. ADE classification
b. ADHM construction
c. AA postulate
d. Ellipse

26. _____ is a non-Euclidean geometry, in which, given a line L and a point p outside L, there exists no line parallel to L passing through p. _____, like hyperbolic geometry, violates Euclid's parallel postulate, which can be interpreted as asserting that there is exactly one line parallel to L passing through p. In _____, there are no parallel lines at all.

a. AA postulate
b. Elliptic Geometry
c. Adjacent angles
d. Absolute geometry

Chapter 6. INEQUALITIES IN GEOMETRY

27. In chemistry, the _____ molecular geometry describes the arrangement of three or more atoms placed at an expected bond angle of 180°. _____ organic molecules, e.g. acetylene, are often described by invoking sp orbital hybridization for the carbon centers. Many _____ molecules exist, prominent examples include CO_2, HCN, and xenon difluoride.
   a. -module
   b. 11-cell
   c. 1-center problem
   d. Linear

28. where a is any scalar. A function which satisfies these properties is called a linear function, or more generally a linear map. This property makes _____ s particularly easy to solve and reason about.
   a. 1-center problem
   b. 11-cell
   c. -module
   d. Linear equation

Chapter 7. SIMILAR POLYGONS

1. A _____ is an expression which compares quantities relative to each other. The most common examples involve two quantities, but in theory any number of quantities can be compared. In mathematical terms, they are represented by separating each quantity with a colon, for example the _____ 2:3, which is read as the _____ 'two to three'.

   a. -module
   b. Slope
   c. Ratio
   d. Slope of a line

2. In linear algebra, a (linear) _____ is a subset of a vector space that is closed under multiplication by positive scalars. In other words, a subset C of a real vector space V is a _____ if and only if >λx belongs to C for any x in C and any positive scalar >λ of V (or, more succintly, if and only if >λC = C for any positive scalar >λ.)

   A _____ is said to be pointed if it includes the null vector (origin) 0; otherwise it is said to be blunt.

   a. Prismatic surface
   b. Cone
   c. Centerpoint
   d. Complex line

3. A _____ is one of the basic shapes of geometry: a polygon with three corners or vertices and three sides or edges which are line segments. A _____ with vertices A, B, and C is denoted ABC.

   In Euclidean geometry any three non-collinear points determine a unique _____ and a unique plane (i.e. a two-dimensional Euclidean space.)

   a. 11-cell
   b. Triangle
   c. -module
   d. 1-center problem

Chapter 7. SIMILAR POLYGONS

4. A timeline of _____ and geometry

- ca. 2000 BC -- Scotland, Carved Stone Balls exhibit a variety of symmetries including all of the symmetries of Platonic solids.
- 1800 BC -- Moscow Mathematical Papyrus, findings volume of a frustum
- 1650 BC -- Rhind Mathematical Papyrus, copy of a lost scroll from around 1850 BC, the scribe Ahmes presents one of the first known approximate values of π at 3.16, the first attempt at squaring the circle, earliest known use of a sort of cotangent, and knowledge of solving first order linear equations
- 1300 BC -- Berlin papyrus (19th dynasty) contains a quadratic equation and its solution.
- 800 BC -- Baudhayana, author of the Baudhayana Sulba Sutra, a Vedic Sanskrit geometric text, contains quadratic equations, and calculates the square root of 2 correct to five decimal places
- ca. 600 BC -- the other Vedic 'Sulba Sutras' use Pythagorean triples, contain of a number of geometrical proofs, and approximate π at 3.16
- 5th century BC -- Hippocrates of Chios utilizes lunes in an attempt to square the circle
- 5th century BC -- Apastamba, author of the Apastamba Sulba Sutra, another Vedic Sanskrit geometric text, makes an attempt at squaring the circle and also calculates the square root of 2 correct to five decimal places
- 530 BC -- Pythagoras studies propositional geometry and vibrating lyre strings; his group also discover the irrationality of the square root of two,
- 370 BC -- Eudoxus states the method of exhaustion for area determination
- 300 BC -- Euclid in his Elements studies geometry as an axiomatic system, proves the infinitude of prime numbers and presents the Euclidean algorithm; he states the law of reflection in Catoptrics, and he proves the fundamental theorem of arithmetic
- 260 BC -- Archimedes proved that the value of π lies between 3 + 1/7 and 3 + 10/71 (approx. 3.1408), that the area of a circle was equal to π multiplied by the square of the radius of the circle and that the area enclosed by a parabola and a straight line is 4/3 multiplied by the area of a triangle with equal base and height. He also gave a very accurate estimate of the value of the square root of 3.
- 225 BC -- Apollonius of Perga writes On Conic Sections and names the ellipse, parabola, and hyperbola,
- 150 BC -- Jain mathematicians in India write the 'Sthananga Sutra', which contains work on the theory of numbers, arithmetical operations, geometry, operations with fractions, simple equations, cubic equations, quartic equations, and permutations and combinations
- 140 BC -- Hipparchus develops the bases of trigonometry.

- 1st century -- Heron of Alexandria, the earliest fleeting reference to square roots of negative numbers.
- 250 -- Diophantus uses symbols for unknown numbers in terms of syncopated _____, and writes Arithmetica, one of the earliest treatises on _____
- ca. 340 -- Pappus of Alexandria states his hexagon theorem and his centroid theorem
- 500 -- Aryabhata writes the 'Aryabhata-Siddhanta', which first introduces the trigonometric functions and methods of calculating their approximate numerical values. It defines the concepts of sine and cosine, and also contains the earliest tables of sine and cosine values
- 600s -- Bhaskara I gives a rational approximation of the sine function
- 600s -- Brahmagupta invents the method of solving indeterminate equations of the second degree and is the first to use _____ to solve astronomical problems. He also develops methods for calculations of the motions and places of various planets, their rising and setting, conjunctions, and the calculation of eclipses of the sun and the moon
- 628 -- Brahmagupta writes the Brahma-sphuta-siddhanta, where zero is clearly explained, and where the modern place-value Indian numeral system is fully developed. It also gives rules for manipulating both negative and positive numbers, methods for computing square roots, methods of solving linear and quadratic equations, and rules for summing series, Brahmagupta's identity, and the Brahmagupta theorem
- 700s -- Virasena gives explicit rules for the Fibonacci sequence, gives the derivation of the volume of a frustum using an infinite procedure, and also deals with the logarithm to base 2 and knows its laws
- 700s -- Shridhara gives the rule for finding the volume of a sphere and also the formula for solving quadratic equations
- 820 -- Al-Khwarizmi -- Persian mathematician, father of _____, writes the Al-Jabr, later transliterated as _____, which introduces systematic algebraic techniques for solving linear and quadratic equations. Translations of his book on arithmetic will introduce the Hindu-Arabic decimal number system to the Western world in the 12th century.

The term algorithm is also named after him.
- 820 -- Al-Mahani conceived the idea of reducing geometrical problems such as doubling the cube to problems in _____.
- 895 -- Thabit ibn Qurra: the only surviving fragment of his original work contains a chapter on the solution and properties of cubic equations. He also generalized the Pythagorean theorem, and discovered the theorem by which pairs of amicable numbers can be found, .
- ca. 900 -- Abu Kamil of Egypt had begun to understand what we would write in symbols as $x^n \cdot x^m = x^{m+n}$
- 953 -- Al-Karaji is the 'first person to completely free _____ from geometrical operations and to replace them with the arithmetical type of operations which are at the core of _____ today. He was first to define the monomials x, x^2, x^3, â€¦ and 1 / x, 1 / x^2, 1 / x^3, â€¦ and to give rules for products of any two of these. He started a school of _____ which flourished for several hundreds of years'. He also discovered the binomial theorem for integer exponents, which 'was a major factor in the development of numerical analysis based on the decimal system.'
- 975 -- Al-Batani -- Extended the Indian concepts of sine and cosine to other trigonometrical ratios, like tangent, secant and their inverse functions. Derived the formula: $\sin\alpha = \tan\alpha / \sqrt{1+\tan^2\alpha}$ and $\cos\alpha = 1/\sqrt{1+\tan^2\alpha}$.

- ca. 1000 -- AbÅ« Sahl al-QÅ«hÄ« (Kuhi) solves equations higher than the second degree.
- ca. 1000 -- Law of sines is discovered by Muslim mathematicians, but it is uncertain who discovers it first between Abu-Mahmud al-Khujandi, Abu Nasr Mansur, and Abu al-Wafa.
- 1070 -- Omar Khayyám begins to write Treatise on Demonstration of Problems of _____ and classifies cubic equations.
- ca. 1100 -- Omar Khayyám 'gave a complete classification of cubic equations with geometric solutions found by means of intersecting conic sections.' He became the first to find general geometric solutions of cubic equations and laid the foundations for the development of analytic geometry and non-Euclidean geometry. He also extracted roots using the decimal system .
- 1100s -- Bhaskara Acharya writes the 'Bijaganita' , which is the first text that recognizes that a positive number has two square roots
- 1130 -- Al-Samawal gave a definition of _____: '[it is concerned] with operating on unknowns using all the arithmetical tools, in the same way as the arithmetician operates on the known.'
- 1135 -- Sharafeddin Tusi followed al-Khayyam's application of _____ to geometry, and wrote a treatise on cubic equations which 'represents an essential contribution to another _____ which aimed to study curves by means of equations, thus inaugurating the beginning of algebraic geometry.'
- ca. 1250 -- Nasir Al-Din Al-Tusi attempts to develop a form of non-Euclidean geometry.
- 1400s -- Nilakantha Somayaji, a Kerala school mathematician, writes the 'Aryabhatiya Bhasya', which contains work on infinite-series expansions, problems of _____, and spherical geometry

- 1520 -- Scipione dal Ferro develops a method for solving 'depressed' cubic equations (cubic equations without an x^2 term), but does not publish.
- 1535 -- Niccolo Tartaglia independently develops a method for solving depressed cubic equations but also does not publish.
- 1539 -- Gerolamo Cardano learns Tartaglia's method for solving depressed cubics and discovers a method for depressing cubics, thereby creating a method for solving all cubics.
- 1540 -- Lodovico Ferrari solves the quartic equation.

- 1600s - Putumana Somayaji writes the 'Paddhati', which presents a detailed discussion of various trigonometric series
- 1619 - René Descartes discovers analytic geometry (Pierre de Fermat claimed that he also discovered it independently),
- 1619 - Johannes Kepler discovers two of the Kepler-Poinsot polyhedra.
- 1637 - Pierre de Fermat claims to have proven Fermat's Last Theorem in his copy of Diophantus' Arithmetica,
- 1637 - First use of the term imaginary number by René Descartes; it was meant to be derogatory.

- 1722 - Abraham de Moivre states de Moivre's formula connecting trigonometric functions and complex numbers,
- 1733 - Giovanni Gerolamo Saccheri studies what geometry would be like if Euclid's fifth postulate were false,
- 1796 - Carl Friedrich Gauss proves that the regular 17-gon can be constructed using only a compass and straightedge
- 1797 - Caspar Wessel associates vectors with complex numbers and studies complex number operations in geometrical terms,
- 1799 - Carl Friedrich Gauss proves the fundamental theorem of _____,

- 1799 - Paolo Ruffini partially proves the Abel-Ruffini theorem that quintic or higher equations cannot be solved by a general formula,

- 1806 - Louis Poinsot discovers the two remaining Kepler-Poinsot polyhedra.
- 1806 - Jean-Robert Argand publishes proof of the Fundamental theorem of _____ and the Argand diagram,
- 1824 - Niels Henrik Abel partially proves the Abel-Ruffini theorem that the general quintic or higher equations cannot be solved by a general formula involving only arithmetical operations and roots,
- 1829 - Bolyai, Gauss, and Lobachevsky invent hyperbolic non-Euclidean geometry,
- 1832 - Évariste Galois presents a general condition for the solvability of algebraic equations, thereby essentially founding group theory and Galois theory,
- 1837 - Pierre Wantsel proves that doubling the cube and trisecting the angle are impossible with only a compass and straightedge, as well as the full completion of the problem of constructability of regular polygons
- 1843 - William Hamilton discovers the calculus of quaternions and deduces that they are non-commutative,
- 1847 - George Boole formalizes symbolic logic in The Mathematical Analysis of Logic, defining what now is called Boolean _____,
- 1854 - Bernhard Riemann introduces Riemannian geometry,
- 1854 - Arthur Cayley shows that quaternions can be used to represent rotations in four-dimensional space,
- 1858 - August Ferdinand Möbius invents the Möbius strip,
- 1870 - Felix Klein constructs an analytic geometry for Lobachevski's geometry thereby establishing its self-consistency and the logical independence of Euclid's fifth postulate,
- 1873 - Charles Hermite proves that e is transcendental,
- 1878 - Charles Hermite solves the general quintic equation by means of elliptic and modular functions
- 1882 - Ferdinand von Lindemann proves that π is transcendental and that therefore the circle cannot be squared with a compass and straightedge,
- 1882 - Felix Klein invents the Klein bottle,
- 1899 - David Hilbert presents a set of self-consistent geometric axioms in Foundations of Geometry,

- 1901 - Élie Cartan develops the exterior derivative,
- 1905 - Einstein's theory of special relativity.
- 1912 - Luitzen Egbertus Jan Brouwer presents the Brouwer fixed-point theorem,
- 1916 - Einstein's theory of general relativity.
- 1930 - Casimir Kuratowski shows that the three-cottage problem has no solution,
- 1931 - Georges de Rham develops theorems in cohomology and characteristic classes,
- 1933 - Karol Borsuk and Stanislaw Ulam present the Borsuk-Ulam antipodal-point theorem,
- 1955 - H. S. M. Coxeter et al. publish the complete list of uniform polyhedron,
- 1981 - Mikhail Gromov develops the theory of hyperbolic groups, revolutionizing both infinite group theory and global differential geometry,
- 1983 - the classification of finite simple groups, a collaborative work involving some hundred mathematicians and spanning thirty years, is completed,
- 1991 - Alain Connes and John W. Lott develop non-commutative geometry,
- 1998 - Thomas Callister Hales (almost certainly) proves the Kepler conjecture,

- 2003 - Grigori Perelman proves the Poincaré conjecture,
- 2007 - a team of researches throughout North America and Europe used networks of computers to map E8 (mathematics.)

Chapter 7. SIMILAR POLYGONS

a. ADHM construction
b. Algebra
c. AA postulate
d. ADE classification

5. In mathematics, the _____ of a real number is its numerical value without regard to its sign. So, for example, 3 is the _____ of both 3 and −3.

The _____ of a number a is denoted by $|\,a\,|$.

a. ADE classification
b. AA postulate
c. ADHM construction
d. Absolute value

6. _____ are a set of two-dimensional diagrams or drawings used to describe a place or object, or to communicate building or fabrication instructions. Usually _____ are drawn or printed on paper, but they can take the form of a digital file.
a. 1-center problem
b. -module
c. 11-cell
d. Plans

7. One of the meanings of the terms _____ and _____ transformation (also called dilation) of a Euclidean space is a function f from the space into itself that multiplies all distances by the same positive scalar r, so that for any two points x and y we have

$$d(f(x), f(y)) = rd(x,y),$$

where 'd(x,y)' is the Euclidean distance from x to y. Two sets are called similar if one is the image of the other under such a _____.

A special case is a homothetic transformation or central _____: it neither involves rotation nor taking the mirror image.

a. Square lattice
b. Similar
c. Flat
d. Similarity

8. In geometry and trigonometry, an _____ is the figure formed by two rays sharing a common endpoint, called the vertex of the _____. The magnitude of the _____ is the 'amount of rotation' that separates the two rays, and can be measured by considering the length of circular arc swept out when one ray is rotated about the vertex to coincide with the other Where there is no possibility of confusion, the term '_____' is used interchangeably for both the geometric configuration itself and for its angular magnitude (which is simply a numerical quantity.)
a. ADE classification
b. ADHM construction
c. AA postulate
d. Angle

9. A _____ is a path that surrounds an area. The word comes from the Greek peri and meter (measure.) The term may be used either for the path or its length.
a. Complementary angles
b. Multilateration
c. Transversal line
d. Perimeter

Chapter 7. SIMILAR POLYGONS

10. In geometry a _____ is traditionally a plane figure that is bounded by a closed path or circuit, composed of a finite sequence of straight line segments (i.e., by a closed polygonal chain.) These segments are called its edges or sides, and the points where two edges meet are the _____'s vertices or corners. The interior of the _____ is sometimes called its body.
   a. Polygon
   b. Dodecagon
   c. Hexagram
   d. Right triangle

11. A _____ is a number which scales or multiplies with a quantity.

example the _____ for:

a cookie that was only 1 pound got enlarged to a cookie that is 2 pounds therefore the _____ is 2 because you multiplied the 1 pound by 2 to get the 2 pounds.

   a. Line field
   b. Moduli scheme
   c. Tarry point
   d. Scale factor

12. Use of _____ in Real-time imagery. The imaging system calls up the structure of _____ needed for the scene to be created from the database. This is transferred to active memory and finally, to the display system (screen, TV monitors etc) so that the scene can be viewed.
   a. 1-center problem
   b. -module
   c. 11-cell
   d. Polygons

13. Two geometrical objects are called _____ if they both have the same shape. Equivalently and more precisely, one is congruent to the result of a uniform scaling (enlarging or shrinking) of the other. Corresponding sides of _____ polygons are in proportion, and corresponding angles of _____ polygons have the same measure.
   a. Simple polytope
   b. Plane
   c. Similar
   d. Steiner-Lehmus theorem

14. A _____ is a rectangle whose side lengths are in the golden ratio, 1: ☒> (one-to-phi), that is, ☒> or approximately 1:1.618.

A distinctive feature of this shape is that when a square section is removed, the remainder is another _____; that is, with the same proportions as the first. Square removal can be repeated infinitely, in which case corresponding corners of the squares form an infinite sequence of points on the golden spiral, the unique logarithmic spiral with this property.

   a. -module
   b. 1-center problem
   c. 11-cell
   d. Golden rectangle

15. In Euclidean geometry, a _____ is a quadrilateral with four right angles. Equivalently, it is an equiangular quadrilateral, but it is not necessarily equilateral.

Chapter 7. SIMILAR POLYGONS

A _____ with vertices ABCD would be denoted as ABCD.

- All angles are 90 degrees.
- Opposite sides are equal in length.
- Opposite sides are parallel.
- Diagonals are equal in length and bisect each other.

The formula for the perimeter of a _____.

If a _____ has length l and width w

- it has area A = lw
- perimeter P = 2l + 2w = 2(l + w)
- and each diagonal has length $\sqrt{l^2 + w^2}$.

When the length is equal to the width, the _____ is a square.

a. 1-center problem
c. 11-cell
b. -module
d. Rectangle

16. In mathematics and the arts, two quantities are in the _____ if the ratio between the sum of those quantities and the larger one is the same as the ratio between the larger one and the smaller. The _____ is an irrational mathematical constant, approximately 1.6180339887.

The _____ is often denoted by the Greek letter phi (>Φ or >φ). The figure of a golden section illustrates the geometric relationship that defines this constant. Expressed algebraically:

a. 1-center problem
c. Golden Ratio
b. 11-cell
d. -module

17. An _____ describes the structure and behaviour of applications used in a business, focused on how they interact with each other and with users. It is focused on the data consumed and produced by applications rather than their internal structure. In application portfolio management, the applications are usually mapped to business functions and to application platform technologies.

a. ADHM construction
c. AA postulate
b. ADE classification
d. Applications architecture

18. In mathematics, a _____ is a convincing demonstration (within the accepted standards of the field) that some mathematical statement is necessarily true. _____s are obtained from deductive reasoning, rather than from inductive or empirical arguments. That is, a _____ must demonstrate that a statement is true in all cases, without a single exception.

a. Contrapositive
b. Theorem
c. Logical axioms
d. Proof

19. In logic, _____ is a form of proof that establishes the truth or validity of a proposition by demonstrating the truth or validity of the converse of its negated parts.

In other words, to prove by contraposition that $P \Rightarrow Q$, prove that $\neg Q \Rightarrow \neg P$.

a. 1-center problem
b. 11-cell
c. -module
d. Proof by contrapositive

20. In vernacular terms, this states 'If P then Q', or, 'If Socrates is a man then Socrates is human.' In a conditional such as this, P is called the antecedent and Q the consequent. One statement is the _____ of the other just when its antecedent is the negated consequent of the other, and vice-versa. The _____ of the given example statement would be:

$$(\neg Q \rightarrow \neg P)$$

That is, 'If not-Q then not-P', or more clearly, 'If Q is not the case, then P is not the case.' Using our example, this is rendered 'If Socrates is not human, then Socrates is not a man.' This statement is said to be contraposed to the original, and is logically equivalent to it.

a. Theorem
b. Logical axioms
c. Contrapositive
d. Logically equivalent

21. In geometry, a _____ is a convex shape comprising two circular arcs, joined at their endpoints. If the arcs have equal radii, it is called a symmetric _____. The corresponding concave shape is the lune.

a. Trilon
b. Medial axis
c. Lens
d. Squircle

22. In mathematics, the Fibonacci numbers are the following sequence of numbers:

$$0,\ 1,\ 1,\ 2,\ 3,\ 5,\ 8,\ 13,\ 21,\ 34,\ 55,\ 89, \ldots.$$

The first two Fibonacci numbers are 0 and 1, and each remaining number is the sum of the previous two:

$$0 + 1 = 1$$
$$1 + 1 = 2$$
$$1 + 2 = 3$$
$$2 + 3 = 5$$
$$3 + 5 = 8$$
$$5 + 8 = 13$$
$$\vdots$$

Some sources omit the initial 0, instead beginning the sequence with two 1s.

Chapter 7. SIMILAR POLYGONS

In mathematical terms, the sequence F_n of Fibonacci numbers is defined by the recurrence relation

$$F_n = F_{n-1} + F_{n-2},$$

with seed values

$$F_0 = 0 \quad \text{and} \quad F_1 = 1.$$

The _____ is named after Leonardo of Pisa, who was known as Fibonacci (a contraction of filius Bonaccio, 'son of Bonaccio'.) Fibonacci's 1202 book Liber Abaci introduced the sequence to Western European mathematics, although the sequence had been previously described in Indian mathematics.

a. 11-cell
b. Fibonacci sequence
c. -module
d. 1-center problem

23. In mathematics, a _____ is an ordered list of objects Like a set, it contains members, and the number of terms is called the length of the _____. Unlike a set, order matters, and the exact same elements can appear multiple times at different positions in the _____.

a. -module
b. Slope
c. Slope of a line
d. Sequence

24. The _____ is the middle point of a line segment. It is equidistant from both endpoints. The formula for determining the _____ of a segment in the plane, with endpoints and is

$$\left(\frac{x_1 + x_2}{2}, \frac{y_1 + y_2}{2} \right).$$

In three-dimensional Cartesian space, the _____ formula is

$$\left(\frac{x_1 + x_2}{2}, \frac{y_1 + y_2}{2}, \frac{z_1 + z_2}{2} \right).$$

_____ used in algebra 1=rectangles _____ used in algebra 2=triangles _____ used in geometry-circles

- Astrology _____ s
- Median
- Segment bisector
- Numerical Integration

Chapter 7. SIMILAR POLYGONS

   a. Golden angle   b. Quincunx
   c. Parallel postulate   d. Midpoint

25. Determining the _____ segment--also called rectification of a curve--was historically difficult. Although many methods were used for specific curves, the advent of calculus led to a general formula that provides closed-form solutions in some cases.
   a. Length of an irregular arc   b. 1-center problem
   c. -module   d. 11-cell

26. In geometry, an _____ is a closed segment of a differentiable curve in the two-dimensional plane; for example, a circular _____ is a segment of the circumference of a circle. If the _____ segment occupies a great circle (or great ellipse), it is considered a great-_____ segment.

The length of an _____ of a circle with radius r and subtending an angle > (measured in radians) with the circle center -- i.e., the central angle -- equals >.

   a. Almost symplectic manifold   b. Equiangular polygon
   c. Order-4 dodecahedral honeycomb   d. Arc

27. In geometry, bisection is the division of something into two equal or congruent parts, usually by a line, which is then called a bisector. The most often considered types of bisectors are segment bisectors and _____. Bisection of a line segment using a compass and ruler Bisection of an angle using a compass and ruler
   a. Axis of symmetry   b. Angle bisectors
   c. Annulus   d. Inscribed sphere

28. A _____ of a curve is the envelope of a family of congruent circles centered on the curve. It generalises the concept of _____ lines.

It is sometimes called the offset curve but the term 'offset' often refers also to translation.

   a. Cassini oval   b. Cissoid
   c. Parallel   d. Trisectrix of Maclaurin

29. In formal mathematical logic, the concept of a _____ may be taken to mean a formula that can be derived according to the derivation rules of a fixed formal system. The statements of a theory as expressed in a formal language are called its elementary _____s and are said to be true.

The essential property of _____s is that they are derivable using a fixed set of inference rules and axioms without any additional assumptions.

   a. Rule of inference   b. Logical axioms
   c. Proof   d. Theorem

Chapter 7. SIMILAR POLYGONS

30. _____ is a major area of mathematics that has emerged through the development of concepts from geometry and set theory, such as those of space, dimension, shape, transformation and others.

Ideas that are now classified as topological were expressed as early as 1736, and toward the end of the 19th century a distinct discipline developed, called in Latin the geometria situs or analysis situs , and later gaining the modern name of _____. In the middle of the 20th century, this was an important growth area within mathematics.

- a. -module
- b. Topology
- c. Metric space
- d. 1-center problem

31. A function or map from one topological space to another is called _____ if the inverse image of any open set is open. If the function maps the real numbers to the real numbers (both spaces with the Standard Topology), then this definition of _____ is equivalent to the definition of _____ in calculus. If a _____ function is one-to-one and onto and if the inverse of the function is also _____, then the function is called a homeomorphism and the domain of the function is said to be homeomorphic to the range.
- a. Fresnel integrals
- b. Continuous
- c. -module
- d. Metric space

32. In each statement above, a is not equal to b. These relations are known as strict _____. The notation a < b may also be read as 'a is strictly less than b'.
- a. ADE classification
- b. AA postulate
- c. ADHM construction
- d. Inequalities

33. In chemistry, the _____ molecular geometry describes the arrangement of three or more atoms placed at an expected bond angle of 180°. _____ organic molecules, e.g. acetylene, are often described by invoking sp orbital hybridization for the carbon centers. Many _____ molecules exist, prominent examples include CO_2, HCN, and xenon difluoride.
- a. 11-cell
- b. -module
- c. Linear
- d. 1-center problem

34. where a is any scalar. A function which satisfies these properties is called a linear function, or more generally a linear map. This property makes _____s particularly easy to solve and reason about.
- a. -module
- b. 1-center problem
- c. Linear equation
- d. 11-cell

35. In mathematics, an algebraic group G contains a unique maximal normal solvable subgroup; and this subgroup is closed. Its identity component is called the _____ of G.
- a. Radical
- b. Hyperspecial subgroup
- c. Restricted Lie algebra
- d. Strong approximation in linear algebraic groups

Chapter 8. RIGHT TRIANGLES

1. In mathematics, the _____ or Pythagoras' theorem is a relation in Euclidean geometry among the three sides of a right triangle. The theorem is usually written as an equation:

$$a^2 + b^2 = c^2$$

where c represents the length of the hypotenuse, and a and b represent the lengths of the other two sides. In words:

The square of the hypotenuse of a right triangle is equal to the sum of the squares on the other two sides.

   a. 1-center problem
   c. 11-cell
   b. Pythagorean Theorem
   d. -module

2. A _____ is a triangle in which one angle is a right angle.

The side opposite the right angle is called the hypotenuse (side [BC] in the figure below.) In addition, the sides adjacent to the right angle are called legs or catheti (singular: cathetus.)

   a. Right triangle
   c. Stellation
   b. Polygonal chain
   d. Simple polygon

3. One of the meanings of the terms _____ and _____ transformation (also called dilation) of a Euclidean space is a function f from the space into itself that multiplies all distances by the same positive scalar r, so that for any two points x and y we have

$$d(f(x), f(y)) = rd(x, y),$$

where 'd(x,y)' is the Euclidean distance from x to y. Two sets are called similar if one is the image of the other under such a _____.

A special case is a homothetic transformation or central _____: it neither involves rotation nor taking the mirror image.

   a. Similar
   c. Square lattice
   b. Similarity
   d. Flat

4. In formal mathematical logic, the concept of a _____ may be taken to mean a formula that can be derived according to the derivation rules of a fixed formal system. The statements of a theory as expressed in a formal language are called its elementary _____s and are said to be true.

The essential property of _____s is that they are derivable using a fixed set of inference rules and axioms without any additional assumptions.

   a. Proof
   c. Rule of inference
   b. Logical axioms
   d. Theorem

5. A _____ is one of the basic shapes of geometry: a polygon with three corners or vertices and three sides or edges which are line segments. A _____ with vertices A, B, and C is denoted ABC.

In Euclidean geometry any three non-collinear points determine a unique _____ and a unique plane (i.e. a two-dimensional Euclidean space.)

a. 11-cell
c. Triangle
b. 1-center problem
d. -module

Chapter 8. RIGHT TRIANGLES

6. A timeline of _____ and geometry

- ca. 2000 BC -- Scotland, Carved Stone Balls exhibit a variety of symmetries including all of the symmetries of Platonic solids.
- 1800 BC -- Moscow Mathematical Papyrus, findings volume of a frustum
- 1650 BC -- Rhind Mathematical Papyrus, copy of a lost scroll from around 1850 BC, the scribe Ahmes presents one of the first known approximate values of π at 3.16, the first attempt at squaring the circle, earliest known use of a sort of cotangent, and knowledge of solving first order linear equations
- 1300 BC -- Berlin papyrus (19th dynasty) contains a quadratic equation and its solution.

- 800 BC -- Baudhayana, author of the Baudhayana Sulba Sutra, a Vedic Sanskrit geometric text, contains quadratic equations, and calculates the square root of 2 correct to five decimal places
- ca. 600 BC -- the other Vedic 'Sulba Sutras' use Pythagorean triples, contain of a number of geometrical proofs, and approximate π at 3.16
- 5th century BC -- Hippocrates of Chios utilizes lunes in an attempt to square the circle
- 5th century BC -- Apastamba, author of the Apastamba Sulba Sutra, another Vedic Sanskrit geometric text, makes an attempt at squaring the circle and also calculates the square root of 2 correct to five decimal places
- 530 BC -- Pythagoras studies propositional geometry and vibrating lyre strings; his group also discover the irrationality of the square root of two,
- 370 BC -- Eudoxus states the method of exhaustion for area determination
- 300 BC -- Euclid in his Elements studies geometry as an axiomatic system, proves the infinitude of prime numbers and presents the Euclidean algorithm; he states the law of reflection in Catoptrics, and he proves the fundamental theorem of arithmetic
- 260 BC -- Archimedes proved that the value of π lies between 3 + 1/7 and 3 + 10/71 (approx. 3.1408), that the area of a circle was equal to π multiplied by the square of the radius of the circle and that the area enclosed by a parabola and a straight line is 4/3 multiplied by the area of a triangle with equal base and height. He also gave a very accurate estimate of the value of the square root of 3.
- 225 BC -- Apollonius of Perga writes On Conic Sections and names the ellipse, parabola, and hyperbola,
- 150 BC -- Jain mathematicians in India write the 'Sthananga Sutra', which contains work on the theory of numbers, arithmetical operations, geometry, operations with fractions, simple equations, cubic equations, quartic equations, and permutations and combinations
- 140 BC -- Hipparchus develops the bases of trigonometry.

- 1st century -- Heron of Alexandria, the earliest fleeting reference to square roots of negative numbers.
- 250 -- Diophantus uses symbols for unknown numbers in terms of syncopated _____, and writes Arithmetica, one of the earliest treatises on _____
- ca. 340 -- Pappus of Alexandria states his hexagon theorem and his centroid theorem
- 500 -- Aryabhata writes the 'Aryabhata-Siddhanta', which first introduces the trigonometric functions and methods of calculating their approximate numerical values. It defines the concepts of sine and cosine, and also contains the earliest tables of sine and cosine values
- 600s -- Bhaskara I gives a rational approximation of the sine function
- 600s -- Brahmagupta invents the method of solving indeterminate equations of the second degree and is the first to use _____ to solve astronomical problems. He also develops methods for calculations of the motions and places of various planets, their rising and setting, conjunctions, and the calculation of eclipses of the sun and the moon
- 628 -- Brahmagupta writes the Brahma-sphuta-siddhanta, where zero is clearly explained, and where the modern place-value Indian numeral system is fully developed. It also gives rules for manipulating both negative and positive numbers, methods for computing square roots, methods of solving linear and quadratic equations, and rules for summing series, Brahmagupta's identity, and the Brahmagupta theorem
- 700s -- Virasena gives explicit rules for the Fibonacci sequence, gives the derivation of the volume of a frustum using an infinite procedure, and also deals with the logarithm to base 2 and knows its laws
- 700s -- Shridhara gives the rule for finding the volume of a sphere and also the formula for solving quadratic equations
- 820 -- Al-Khwarizmi -- Persian mathematician, father of _____, writes the Al-Jabr, later transliterated as _____, which introduces systematic algebraic techniques for solving linear and quadratic equations. Translations of his book on arithmetic will introduce the Hindu-Arabic decimal number system to the Western world in the 12th century.

The term algorithm is also named after him.
- 820 -- Al-Mahani conceived the idea of reducing geometrical problems such as doubling the cube to problems in _____.
- 895 -- Thabit ibn Qurra: the only surviving fragment of his original work contains a chapter on the solution and properties of cubic equations. He also generalized the Pythagorean theorem, and discovered the theorem by which pairs of amicable numbers can be found, .
- ca. 900 -- Abu Kamil of Egypt had begun to understand what we would write in symbols as $x^n \cdot x^m = x^{m+n}$
- 953 -- Al-Karaji is the 'first person to completely free _____ from geometrical operations and to replace them with the arithmetical type of operations which are at the core of _____ today. He was first to define the monomials x, x^2, x^3, … and 1 / x, 1 / x^2, 1 / x^3, … and to give rules for products of any two of these. He started a school of _____ which flourished for several hundreds of years'. He also discovered the binomial theorem for integer exponents, which 'was a major factor in the development of numerical analysis based on the decimal system.'
- 975 -- Al-Batani -- Extended the Indian concepts of sine and cosine to other trigonometrical ratios, like tangent, secant and their inverse functions. Derived the formula: $\sin\alpha = \tan\alpha / \sqrt{1+\tan^2\alpha}$ and $\cos\alpha = 1/\sqrt{1+\tan^2\alpha}$.

- ca. 1000 -- Abū Sahl al-Qūhī (Kuhi) solves equations higher than the second degree.
- ca. 1000 -- Law of sines is discovered by Muslim mathematicians, but it is uncertain who discovers it first between Abu-Mahmud al-Khujandi, Abu Nasr Mansur, and Abu al-Wafa.
- 1070 -- Omar Khayyám begins to write Treatise on Demonstration of Problems of _____ and classifies cubic equations.
- ca. 1100 -- Omar Khayyám 'gave a complete classification of cubic equations with geometric solutions found by means of intersecting conic sections.' He became the first to find general geometric solutions of cubic equations and laid the foundations for the development of analytic geometry and non-Euclidean geometry. He also extracted roots using the decimal system .
- 1100s -- Bhaskara Acharya writes the 'Bijaganita' , which is the first text that recognizes that a positive number has two square roots
- 1130 -- Al-Samawal gave a definition of _____: '[it is concerned] with operating on unknowns using all the arithmetical tools, in the same way as the arithmetician operates on the known.'
- 1135 -- Sharafeddin Tusi followed al-Khayyam's application of _____ to geometry, and wrote a treatise on cubic equations which 'represents an essential contribution to another _____ which aimed to study curves by means of equations, thus inaugurating the beginning of algebraic geometry.'
- ca. 1250 -- Nasir Al-Din Al-Tusi attempts to develop a form of non-Euclidean geometry.
- 1400s -- Nilakantha Somayaji, a Kerala school mathematician, writes the 'Aryabhatiya Bhasya', which contains work on infinite-series expansions, problems of _____, and spherical geometry

- 1520 -- Scipione dal Ferro develops a method for solving 'depressed' cubic equations (cubic equations without an x^2 term), but does not publish.
- 1535 -- Niccolo Tartaglia independently develops a method for solving depressed cubic equations but also does not publish.
- 1539 -- Gerolamo Cardano learns Tartaglia's method for solving depressed cubics and discovers a method for depressing cubics, thereby creating a method for solving all cubics.
- 1540 -- Lodovico Ferrari solves the quartic equation.

- 1600s - Putumana Somayaji writes the 'Paddhati', which presents a detailed discussion of various trigonometric series
- 1619 - René Descartes discovers analytic geometry (Pierre de Fermat claimed that he also discovered it independently),
- 1619 - Johannes Kepler discovers two of the Kepler-Poinsot polyhedra.
- 1637 - Pierre de Fermat claims to have proven Fermat's Last Theorem in his copy of Diophantus' Arithmetica,
- 1637 - First use of the term imaginary number by René Descartes; it was meant to be derogatory.

- 1722 - Abraham de Moivre states de Moivre's formula connecting trigonometric functions and complex numbers,
- 1733 - Giovanni Gerolamo Saccheri studies what geometry would be like if Euclid's fifth postulate were false,
- 1796 - Carl Friedrich Gauss proves that the regular 17-gon can be constructed using only a compass and straightedge
- 1797 - Caspar Wessel associates vectors with complex numbers and studies complex number operations in geometrical terms,
- 1799 - Carl Friedrich Gauss proves the fundamental theorem of _____,

- 1799 - Paolo Ruffini partially proves the Abel-Ruffini theorem that quintic or higher equations cannot be solved by a general formula,

- 1806 - Louis Poinsot discovers the two remaining Kepler-Poinsot polyhedra.
- 1806 - Jean-Robert Argand publishes proof of the Fundamental theorem of _____ and the Argand diagram,
- 1824 - Niels Henrik Abel partially proves the Abel-Ruffini theorem that the general quintic or higher equations cannot be solved by a general formula involving only arithmetical operations and roots,
- 1829 - Bolyai, Gauss, and Lobachevsky invent hyperbolic non-Euclidean geometry,
- 1832 - Évariste Galois presents a general condition for the solvability of algebraic equations, thereby essentially founding group theory and Galois theory,
- 1837 - Pierre Wantsel proves that doubling the cube and trisecting the angle are impossible with only a compass and straightedge, as well as the full completion of the problem of constructability of regular polygons
- 1843 - William Hamilton discovers the calculus of quaternions and deduces that they are non-commutative,
- 1847 - George Boole formalizes symbolic logic in The Mathematical Analysis of Logic, defining what now is called Boolean _____,
- 1854 - Bernhard Riemann introduces Riemannian geometry,
- 1854 - Arthur Cayley shows that quaternions can be used to represent rotations in four-dimensional space,
- 1858 - August Ferdinand Möbius invents the Möbius strip,
- 1870 - Felix Klein constructs an analytic geometry for Lobachevski's geometry thereby establishing its self-consistency and the logical independence of Euclid's fifth postulate,
- 1873 - Charles Hermite proves that e is transcendental,
- 1878 - Charles Hermite solves the general quintic equation by means of elliptic and modular functions
- 1882 - Ferdinand von Lindemann proves that π is transcendental and that therefore the circle cannot be squared with a compass and straightedge,
- 1882 - Felix Klein invents the Klein bottle,
- 1899 - David Hilbert presents a set of self-consistent geometric axioms in Foundations of Geometry,

- 1901 - Élie Cartan develops the exterior derivative,
- 1905 - Einstein's theory of special relativity.
- 1912 - Luitzen Egbertus Jan Brouwer presents the Brouwer fixed-point theorem,
- 1916 - Einstein's theory of general relativity.
- 1930 - Casimir Kuratowski shows that the three-cottage problem has no solution,
- 1931 - Georges de Rham develops theorems in cohomology and characteristic classes,
- 1933 - Karol Borsuk and Stanislaw Ulam present the Borsuk-Ulam antipodal-point theorem,
- 1955 - H. S. M. Coxeter et al. publish the complete list of uniform polyhedron,
- 1981 - Mikhail Gromov develops the theory of hyperbolic groups, revolutionizing both infinite group theory and global differential geometry,
- 1983 - the classification of finite simple groups, a collaborative work involving some hundred mathematicians and spanning thirty years, is completed,
- 1991 - Alain Connes and John W. Lott develop non-commutative geometry,
- 1998 - Thomas Callister Hales (almost certainly) proves the Kepler conjecture,

- 2003 - Grigori Perelman proves the Poincaré conjecture,
- 2007 - a team of researches throughout North America and Europe used networks of computers to map E8 (mathematics.)

Chapter 8. RIGHT TRIANGLES

a. AA postulate
b. ADHM construction
c. Algebra
d. ADE classification

7. In mathematics, an algebraic group G contains a unique maximal normal solvable subgroup; and this subgroup is closed. Its identity component is called the _____ of G.
   a. Restricted Lie algebra
   b. Radical
   c. Hyperspecial subgroup
   d. Strong approximation in linear algebraic groups

8. In mathematics, the _____ of a real number is its numerical value without regard to its sign. So, for example, 3 is the _____ of both 3 and −3.

The _____ of a number a is denoted by $|a|$.

   a. AA postulate
   b. ADE classification
   c. ADHM construction
   d. Absolute value

9. In geometry a _____ is traditionally a plane figure that is bounded by a closed path or circuit, composed of a finite sequence of straight line segments (i.e., by a closed polygonal chain.) These segments are called its edges or sides, and the points where two edges meet are the _____'s vertices or corners. The interior of the _____ is sometimes called its body.
   a. Polygon
   b. Right triangle
   c. Hexagram
   d. Dodecagon

10. A _____ is a building where the outer surfaces are triangular and converge at a point. The base of a _____ is usually trilateral or quadrilateral (but may be of any polygon shape), meaning that a _____ usually has four or five faces. A _____'s design, with the majority of the weight closer to the ground, means that less material higher up on the _____ will be pushing down from above: this allowed early civilizations to create stable monumental structures.
    a. -module
    b. Pyramid
    c. 11-cell
    d. 1-center problem

11. In Euclidean geometry, a _____ is a regular quadrilateral. This means that it has four equal sides and four equal angles (90 degree angles, or right angles.) A _____ with vertices ABCD would be denoted ABCD.
    a. 1-center problem
    b. 11-cell
    c. -module
    d. Square

12.

A _____ consists of three positive integers a, b, and c, such that $a^2 + b^2 = c^2$. Such a triple is commonly written (a, b, c), and a well-known example is (3, 4, 5). If (a, b, c) is a _____, then so is (ka, kb, kc) for any positive integer k.

   a. Pythagorean quadruple
   b. -module
   c. 1-center problem
   d. Pythagorean triple

13. A _____ of a curve is the envelope of a family of congruent circles centered on the curve. It generalises the concept of _____ lines.

Chapter 8. RIGHT TRIANGLES

It is sometimes called the offset curve but the term 'offset' often refers also to translation.

a. Trisectrix of Maclaurin
b. Cassini oval
c. Cissoid
d. Parallel

14. In geometry, the _____ is a distinctive axiom in what is now called Euclidean geometry. It states that:

If a line segment intersects two straight lines forming two interior angles on the same side that sum to less than two right angles, then the two lines, if extended indefinitely, meet on that side on which the angles sum to less than two right angles.

Euclidean geometry is the study of geometry that satisfies all of Euclid's axioms, including the _____.

a. Concyclic points
b. Hypotenuse
c. Confocal
d. Parallel Postulate

15. In mathematics, _____ geometry describes hyperbolic and elliptic geometry, which are contrasted with Euclidean geometry. The essential difference between Euclidean and _____ geometry is the nature of parallel lines. Euclid's fifth postulate, the parallel postulate, is equivalent to Playfair's postulate, which states that, within a two-dimensional plane, for any given line l and a point A, which is not on l, there is exactly one line through A that does not intersect l.

a. Codimension
b. Coaxial
c. Coplanar
d. Non-Euclidean

16. In geometry, two sets of points are called _____ if one can be transformed into the other by an isometry, i.e., a combination of translations, rotations and reflections. Less formally, two figures are _____ if they have the same shape and size, but are in different positions (for instance one may be rotated, flipped, or simply placed somewhere else).

a. 1-center problem
b. 11-cell
c. -module
d. Congruent

17. A _____ is an expression which compares quantities relative to each other. The most common examples involve two quantities, but in theory any number of quantities can be compared. In mathematical terms, they are represented by separating each quantity with a colon, for example the _____ 2:3, which is read as the _____ 'two to three'.

a. -module
b. Slope
c. Slope of a line
d. Ratio

18. In geometry, the _____ line (or simply the _____) to a curve at a given point is the straight line that 'just touches' the curve at that point (in the sense explained more precisely below.) As it passes through the point of tangency, the _____ line is 'going in the same direction' as the curve, and in this sense it is the best straight-line approximation to the curve at that point. The same definition applies to space curves and curves in n-dimensional Euclidean space.

a. Measuring function
b. Cartan connection
c. Tangent
d. Metric signature

19. _____ is a branch of mathematics that deals with triangles, particularly those plane triangles in which one angle has 90 degrees (right triangles) _____ deals with relationships between the sides and the angles of triangles and with the trigonometric functions, which describe those relationships.

_____ has applications in both pure mathematics and in applied mathematics, where it is essential in many branches of science and technology.

a. -module
b. 1-center problem
c. Trigonometry
d. Trigonometric

20. Trigonometry is a branch of mathematics that deals with triangles, particularly those plane triangles in which one angle has 90 degrees (right triangles.) Trigonometry deals with relationships between the sides and the angles of triangles and with the _____ functions, which describe those relationships.

Trigonometry has applications in both pure mathematics and in applied mathematics, where it is essential in many branches of science and technology.

a. -module
b. 1-center problem
c. Trigonometry
d. Trigonometric

21. The _____ of any physical feature such as a hill, stream, roof, railroad refers to the amount of inclination of that surface where zero indicates level (with respect to gravity) and larger numbers indicate higher degrees of 'tilt'. Often slope is calculated as a ratio of 'rise over run' in which run is the horizontal distance and rise is the vertical distance.
a. Grade
b. -module
c. 11-cell
d. 1-center problem

22. An _____ describes the structure and behaviour of applications used in a business, focused on how they interact with each other and with users. It is focused on the data consumed and produced by applications rather than their internal structure. In application portfolio management, the applications are usually mapped to business functions and to application platform technologies.
a. ADE classification
b. ADHM construction
c. AA postulate
d. Applications architecture

23. In mathematics, a _____ or distance function is a function which defines a distance between elements of a set. A set with a _____ is called a _____ space. A _____ induces a topology on a set but not all topologies can be generated by a _____.
a. Comparison triangle
b. Polyhedral space
c. Systolic inequalities for curves on surfaces
d. Metric

24. In geometry and trigonometry, an _____ is the figure formed by two rays sharing a common endpoint, called the vertex of the _____ . The magnitude of the _____ is the 'amount of rotation' that separates the two rays, and can be measured by considering the length of circular arc swept out when one ray is rotated about the vertex to coincide with the other Where there is no possibility of confusion, the term '_____' is used interchangeably for both the geometric configuration itself and for its angular magnitude (which is simply a numerical quantity.)
a. ADE classification
b. ADHM construction
c. AA postulate
d. Angle

25. The _____ of a geographic location is its height above a fixed reference point, often the mean sea level. _____, or geometric height, is mainly used when referring to points on the Earth's surface, while altitude or geopotential height is used for points above the surface, such as an aircraft in flight or a spacecraft in orbit.

Less commonly, _____ is measured using the center of the Earth as the reference point.

   a. ADE classification
   c. ADHM construction
   b. AA postulate
   d. Elevation

Chapter 9. CIRCLES

1. A _____ of a curve is a geometric line segment whose endpoints both lie on the curve. A secant or a secant line is the line extension of a _____. The red line BX is a _____.

Among properties of _____s of a circle are the following:

1. _____s are equidistant from the center if and only if their lengths are equal.
2. A _____'s perpendicular bisector passes through the centre.
3. If the line extensions (secant lines) of _____s AB and CD intersect at a point P, then their lengths satisfy APÂ·PB = CPÂ·PD (power of a point theorem.)

The area that a circular _____ 'cuts off' is called a circular segment.

_____s were used extensively in the early development of trigonometry.

  a. Trisectrix of Maclaurin   b. Harmonograph
  c. Positively oriented curve   d. Chord

2. A _____ is a simple shape of Euclidean geometry consisting of those points in a plane which are the same distance from a given point called the centre. The common distance of the points of a _____ from its center is called its radius.

_____s are simple closed curves which divide the plane into two regions, an interior and an exterior.

  a. 11-cell   b. 1-center problem
  c. -module   d. Circle

3. In geometry, a _____ of a circle is any straight line segment that passes through the center of the circle and whose endpoints are on the circle. The _____s are the longest chords of the circle. The word '_____' derives from Greek >δ>ιÎ¬>μ>ε>τ>ρ>ο>ς , 'diagonal of a circle', from >δ>ι>α- (dia-), 'across, through' + >μÎ>τ>ρ>ο>ν (metron), 'a measure'.)
  a. Diameter   b. Line
  c. Bisection   d. Hypotenuse

4. In geometry, topology and related branches of mathematics a spatial _____ describes a specific object within a given space that consists of neither volume, area, length, nor any other higher dimensional analogue. Thus, a _____ is a 0-dimensional object. Because of their nature as one of the simplest geometric concepts, they are often used in one form or another as the fundamental constituents of geometry, physics, vector graphics, and many other fields.
  a. -module   b. 1-center problem
  c. 11-cell   d. Point

5. In geometry, the tangent line (or simply the tangent) to a curve at a given point is the straight line that 'just touches' the curve at that point (in the sense explained more precisely below.) As it passes through the _____, the tangent line is 'going in the same direction' as the curve, and in this sense it is the best straight-line approximation to the curve at that point. The same definition applies to space curves and curves in n-dimensional Euclidean space.
  a. Pedal curve   b. Symmetric space
  c. Point of tangency   d. Bochner identity

Chapter 9. CIRCLES

6. In every _____ there is a cuboid with all vertices tangent to the surface of said _____. It immediately becomes apparent that the cuboid inscribed in the _____ must be a cube with all vertices tangent to the surface of the _____.

Formula 1, shown below, finds the length of one side of the inscribed cube, and Formula 2 finds the volume of the inscribed cube.

    a. Cone   b. Circumference
    c. Sphere   d. Point group in two dimensions

7. In geometry, the _____ line (or simply the _____) to a curve at a given point is the straight line that 'just touches' the curve at that point (in the sense explained more precisely below.) As it passes through the point of tangency, the _____ line is 'going in the same direction' as the curve, and in this sense it is the best straight-line approximation to the curve at that point. The same definition applies to space curves and curves in n-dimensional Euclidean space.

    a. Tangent   b. Metric signature
    c. Cartan connection   d. Measuring function

8. In geometry, an _____ is a closed segment of a differentiable curve in the two-dimensional plane; for example, a circular _____ is a segment of the circumference of a circle. If the _____ segment occupies a great circle (or great ellipse), it is considered a great-_____ segment.

The length of an _____ of a circle with radius r and subtending an angle ☐> (measured in radians) with the circle center -- i.e., the central angle -- equals ☐>.

    a. Equiangular polygon   b. Arc
    c. Order-4 dodecahedral honeycomb   d. Almost symplectic manifold

9. In geometry, two sets of points are called _____ if one can be transformed into the other by an isometry, i.e., a combination of translations, rotations and reflections. Less formally, two figures are _____ if they have the same shape and size, but are in different positions (for instance one may be rotated, flipped, or simply placed somewhere else).

    a. 1-center problem   b. -module
    c. Congruent   d. 11-cell

10. In geometry a _____ is traditionally a plane figure that is bounded by a closed path or circuit, composed of a finite sequence of straight line segments (i.e., by a closed polygonal chain.) These segments are called its edges or sides, and the points where two edges meet are the _____'s vertices or corners. The interior of the _____ is sometimes called its body.

    a. Dodecagon   b. Right triangle
    c. Hexagram   d. Polygon

11. In geometry, the _____ circle or circumcircle of a polygon is a circle which passes through all the vertices of the polygon. The center of this circle is called the circumcenter.

A polygon which has a _____ circle is called a cyclic polygon.

Chapter 9. CIRCLES

a. Circle sector
b. Circumcenter
c. Circumscribed
d. Circular sector

12. _____ objects share the same center, axis or origin with one inside the other. Circles, tubes, cylindrical shafts, disks, and spheres may be _____ to one another. _____ objects do not generally have the same radius.
   a. Cell
   b. Tropical geometry
   c. Concentric
   d. Miller indices

13. In geometry, an _____ planar shape or solid is one that is enclosed by and 'fits snugly' inside another geometric shape or solid. Specifically, at all points where figures meet, their edges must lie tangent. There must be no object similar to the _____ object but larger and also enclosed by the outer figure.
   a. Octomino
   b. Order-4 dodecahedral honeycomb
   c. Inscribed
   d. Isometry group

14. A _____ of a sphere is a circle that runs along the surface of that sphere so as to cut it into two equal halves. The _____ therefore has both the same circumference and the same center as the sphere. It is the largest circle that can be drawn on a given sphere.
   a. Great circle
   b. Conway polyhedron notation
   c. Line segment
   d. Complementary angles

15. In geometry and trigonometry, an _____ is the figure formed by two rays sharing a common endpoint, called the vertex of the _____ . The magnitude of the _____ is the 'amount of rotation' that separates the two rays, and can be measured by considering the length of circular arc swept out when one ray is rotated about the vertex to coincide with the other Where there is no possibility of confusion, the term '_____' is used interchangeably for both the geometric configuration itself and for its angular magnitude (which is simply a numerical quantity.)
   a. Angle
   b. ADHM construction
   c. AA postulate
   d. ADE classification

16. In mathematics (more specifically geometry), a _____ is a two-dimensional geometric shape that forms half of a circle. Being half of a circle's 360°, the arc of a _____ always measures 180°. A triangle inscribed in a _____ is always a right triangle.
   a. Confocal
   b. Semicircle
   c. Hypotenuse
   d. Line

17. _____ is an adjective meaning contiguous, adjoining or abutting.

In geometry, _____ is when sides meet to make an angle.

In trigonometry the _____ side of a right angled triangle is the cathetus next to the angle in question.

   a. Ambient space
   b. Equidimensional
   c. Edge figure
   d. Adjacent

18. A timeline of _____ and geometry

- ca. 2000 BC -- Scotland, Carved Stone Balls exhibit a variety of symmetries including all of the symmetries of Platonic solids.
- 1800 BC -- Moscow Mathematical Papyrus, findings volume of a frustum
- 1650 BC -- Rhind Mathematical Papyrus, copy of a lost scroll from around 1850 BC, the scribe Ahmes presents one of the first known approximate values of π at 3.16, the first attempt at squaring the circle, earliest known use of a sort of cotangent, and knowledge of solving first order linear equations
- 1300 BC -- Berlin papyrus (19th dynasty) contains a quadratic equation and its solution.

- 800 BC -- Baudhayana, author of the Baudhayana Sulba Sutra, a Vedic Sanskrit geometric text, contains quadratic equations, and calculates the square root of 2 correct to five decimal places
- ca. 600 BC -- the other Vedic 'Sulba Sutras' use Pythagorean triples, contain of a number of geometrical proofs, and approximate π at 3.16
- 5th century BC -- Hippocrates of Chios utilizes lunes in an attempt to square the circle
- 5th century BC -- Apastamba, author of the Apastamba Sulba Sutra, another Vedic Sanskrit geometric text, makes an attempt at squaring the circle and also calculates the square root of 2 correct to five decimal places
- 530 BC -- Pythagoras studies propositional geometry and vibrating lyre strings; his group also discover the irrationality of the square root of two,
- 370 BC -- Eudoxus states the method of exhaustion for area determination
- 300 BC -- Euclid in his Elements studies geometry as an axiomatic system, proves the infinitude of prime numbers and presents the Euclidean algorithm; he states the law of reflection in Catoptrics, and he proves the fundamental theorem of arithmetic
- 260 BC -- Archimedes proved that the value of π lies between 3 + 1/7 and 3 + 10/71 (approx. 3.1408), that the area of a circle was equal to π multiplied by the square of the radius of the circle and that the area enclosed by a parabola and a straight line is 4/3 multiplied by the area of a triangle with equal base and height. He also gave a very accurate estimate of the value of the square root of 3.
- 225 BC -- Apollonius of Perga writes On Conic Sections and names the ellipse, parabola, and hyperbola,
- 150 BC -- Jain mathematicians in India write the 'Sthananga Sutra', which contains work on the theory of numbers, arithmetical operations, geometry, operations with fractions, simple equations, cubic equations, quartic equations, and permutations and combinations
- 140 BC -- Hipparchus develops the bases of trigonometry.

- 1st century -- Heron of Alexandria, the earliest fleeting reference to square roots of negative numbers.
- 250 -- Diophantus uses symbols for unknown numbers in terms of syncopated _____, and writes Arithmetica, one of the earliest treatises on _____
- ca. 340 -- Pappus of Alexandria states his hexagon theorem and his centroid theorem
- 500 -- Aryabhata writes the 'Aryabhata-Siddhanta', which first introduces the trigonometric functions and methods of calculating their approximate numerical values. It defines the concepts of sine and cosine, and also contains the earliest tables of sine and cosine values
- 600s -- Bhaskara I gives a rational approximation of the sine function
- 600s -- Brahmagupta invents the method of solving indeterminate equations of the second degree and is the first to use _____ to solve astronomical problems. He also develops methods for calculations of the motions and places of various planets, their rising and setting, conjunctions, and the calculation of eclipses of the sun and the moon
- 628 -- Brahmagupta writes the Brahma-sphuta-siddhanta, where zero is clearly explained, and where the modern place-value Indian numeral system is fully developed. It also gives rules for manipulating both negative and positive numbers, methods for computing square roots, methods of solving linear and quadratic equations, and rules for summing series, Brahmagupta's identity, and the Brahmagupta theorem
- 700s -- Virasena gives explicit rules for the Fibonacci sequence, gives the derivation of the volume of a frustum using an infinite procedure, and also deals with the logarithm to base 2 and knows its laws
- 700s -- Shridhara gives the rule for finding the volume of a sphere and also the formula for solving quadratic equations
- 820 -- Al-Khwarizmi -- Persian mathematician, father of _____, writes the Al-Jabr, later transliterated as _____, which introduces systematic algebraic techniques for solving linear and quadratic equations. Translations of his book on arithmetic will introduce the Hindu-Arabic decimal number system to the Western world in the 12th century.

- The term algorithm is also named after him.
- 820 -- Al-Mahani conceived the idea of reducing geometrical problems such as doubling the cube to problems in _____.
- 895 -- Thabit ibn Qurra: the only surviving fragment of his original work contains a chapter on the solution and properties of cubic equations. He also generalized the Pythagorean theorem, and discovered the theorem by which pairs of amicable numbers can be found, .
- ca. 900 -- Abu Kamil of Egypt had begun to understand what we would write in symbols as $x^n \cdot x^m = x^{m+n}$
- 953 -- Al-Karaji is the 'first person to completely free _____ from geometrical operations and to replace them with the arithmetical type of operations which are at the core of _____ today. He was first to define the monomials x, x^2, x^3, â€¦ and 1 / x, 1 / x^2, 1 / x^3, â€¦ and to give rules for products of any two of these. He started a school of _____ which flourished for several hundreds of years'. He also discovered the binomial theorem for integer exponents, which 'was a major factor in the development of numerical analysis based on the decimal system.'
- 975 -- Al-Batani -- Extended the Indian concepts of sine and cosine to other trigonometrical ratios, like tangent, secant and their inverse functions. Derived the formula: $\sin\alpha = \tan\alpha/\sqrt{1+\tan^2\alpha}$ and $\cos\alpha = 1/\sqrt{1+\tan^2\alpha}$.

- ca. 1000 -- AbÅ« Sahl al-QÅ«hÄ« (Kuhi) solves equations higher than the second degree.
- ca. 1000 -- Law of sines is discovered by Muslim mathematicians, but it is uncertain who discovers it first between Abu-Mahmud al-Khujandi, Abu Nasr Mansur, and Abu al-Wafa.
- 1070 -- Omar Khayyám begins to write Treatise on Demonstration of Problems of _____ and classifies cubic equations.
- ca. 1100 -- Omar Khayyám 'gave a complete classification of cubic equations with geometric solutions found by means of intersecting conic sections.' He became the first to find general geometric solutions of cubic equations and laid the foundations for the development of analytic geometry and non-Euclidean geometry. He also extracted roots using the decimal system .
- 1100s -- Bhaskara Acharya writes the 'Bijaganita' , which is the first text that recognizes that a positive number has two square roots
- 1130 -- Al-Samawal gave a definition of _____: '[it is concerned] with operating on unknowns using all the arithmetical tools, in the same way as the arithmetician operates on the known.'
- 1135 -- Sharafeddin Tusi followed al-Khayyam's application of _____ to geometry, and wrote a treatise on cubic equations which 'represents an essential contribution to another _____ which aimed to study curves by means of equations, thus inaugurating the beginning of algebraic geometry.'
- ca. 1250 -- Nasir Al-Din Al-Tusi attempts to develop a form of non-Euclidean geometry.
- 1400s -- Nilakantha Somayaji, a Kerala school mathematician, writes the 'Aryabhatiya Bhasya', which contains work on infinite-series expansions, problems of _____, and spherical geometry

- 1520 -- Scipione dal Ferro develops a method for solving 'depressed' cubic equations (cubic equations without an x^2 term), but does not publish.
- 1535 -- Niccolo Tartaglia independently develops a method for solving depressed cubic equations but also does not publish.
- 1539 -- Gerolamo Cardano learns Tartaglia's method for solving depressed cubics and discovers a method for depressing cubics, thereby creating a method for solving all cubics.
- 1540 -- Lodovico Ferrari solves the quartic equation.

- 1600s - Putumana Somayaji writes the 'Paddhati', which presents a detailed discussion of various trigonometric series
- 1619 - René Descartes discovers analytic geometry (Pierre de Fermat claimed that he also discovered it independently),
- 1619 - Johannes Kepler discovers two of the Kepler-Poinsot polyhedra.
- 1637 - Pierre de Fermat claims to have proven Fermat's Last Theorem in his copy of Diophantus' Arithmetica,
- 1637 - First use of the term imaginary number by René Descartes; it was meant to be derogatory.

- 1722 - Abraham de Moivre states de Moivre's formula connecting trigonometric functions and complex numbers,
- 1733 - Giovanni Gerolamo Saccheri studies what geometry would be like if Euclid's fifth postulate were false,
- 1796 - Carl Friedrich Gauss proves that the regular 17-gon can be constructed using only a compass and straightedge
- 1797 - Caspar Wessel associates vectors with complex numbers and studies complex number operations in geometrical terms,
- 1799 - Carl Friedrich Gauss proves the fundamental theorem of _____,

- 1799 - Paolo Ruffini partially proves the Abel-Ruffini theorem that quintic or higher equations cannot be solved by a general formula,

- 1806 - Louis Poinsot discovers the two remaining Kepler-Poinsot polyhedra.
- 1806 - Jean-Robert Argand publishes proof of the Fundamental theorem of _____ and the Argand diagram,
- 1824 - Niels Henrik Abel partially proves the Abel-Ruffini theorem that the general quintic or higher equations cannot be solved by a general formula involving only arithmetical operations and roots,
- 1829 - Bolyai, Gauss, and Lobachevsky invent hyperbolic non-Euclidean geometry,
- 1832 - Évariste Galois presents a general condition for the solvability of algebraic equations, thereby essentially founding group theory and Galois theory,
- 1837 - Pierre Wantsel proves that doubling the cube and trisecting the angle are impossible with only a compass and straightedge, as well as the full completion of the problem of constructability of regular polygons
- 1843 - William Hamilton discovers the calculus of quaternions and deduces that they are non-commutative,
- 1847 - George Boole formalizes symbolic logic in The Mathematical Analysis of Logic, defining what now is called Boolean _____,
- 1854 - Bernhard Riemann introduces Riemannian geometry,
- 1854 - Arthur Cayley shows that quaternions can be used to represent rotations in four-dimensional space,
- 1858 - August Ferdinand Möbius invents the Möbius strip,
- 1870 - Felix Klein constructs an analytic geometry for Lobachevski's geometry thereby establishing its self-consistency and the logical independence of Euclid's fifth postulate,
- 1873 - Charles Hermite proves that e is transcendental,
- 1878 - Charles Hermite solves the general quintic equation by means of elliptic and modular functions
- 1882 - Ferdinand von Lindemann proves that π is transcendental and that therefore the circle cannot be squared with a compass and straightedge,
- 1882 - Felix Klein invents the Klein bottle,
- 1899 - David Hilbert presents a set of self-consistent geometric axioms in Foundations of Geometry,

- 1901 - Élie Cartan develops the exterior derivative,
- 1905 - Einstein's theory of special relativity.
- 1912 - Luitzen Egbertus Jan Brouwer presents the Brouwer fixed-point theorem,
- 1916 - Einstein's theory of general relativity.
- 1930 - Casimir Kuratowski shows that the three-cottage problem has no solution,
- 1931 - Georges de Rham develops theorems in cohomology and characteristic classes,
- 1933 - Karol Borsuk and Stanislaw Ulam present the Borsuk-Ulam antipodal-point theorem,
- 1955 - H. S. M. Coxeter et al. publish the complete list of uniform polyhedron,
- 1981 - Mikhail Gromov develops the theory of hyperbolic groups, revolutionizing both infinite group theory and global differential geometry,
- 1983 - the classification of finite simple groups, a collaborative work involving some hundred mathematicians and spanning thirty years, is completed,
- 1991 - Alain Connes and John W. Lott develop non-commutative geometry,
- 1998 - Thomas Callister Hales (almost certainly) proves the Kepler conjecture,

- 2003 - Grigori Perelman proves the Poincaré conjecture,
- 2007 - a team of researches throughout North America and Europe used networks of computers to map E8 (mathematics.)

Chapter 9. CIRCLES

a. Algebra
b. ADHM construction
c. AA postulate
d. ADE classification

19. A _____ is an angle whose vertex is the center of a circle, and whose sides pass through a pair of points on the circle, thereby subtending an arc between those two points whose angle is (by definition) equal to the _____ itself. It is also known as the arc segment's angular distance.

On a sphere or ellipsoid, the _____ is delineated along a great circle.

a. Cuboid
b. Central Angle
c. Spidron
d. Skew lines

20. An _____ describes the structure and behaviour of applications used in a business, focused on how they interact with each other and with users. It is focused on the data consumed and produced by applications rather than their internal structure. In application portfolio management, the applications are usually mapped to business functions and to application platform technologies.
a. AA postulate
b. ADHM construction
c. ADE classification
d. Applications architecture

21. In geometry, an _____ is formed when two secant lines of a circle (or, in a degenerate case, when one secant line and one tangent line of that circle) intersect on the circle.

Typically, it is easiest to think of an _____ as being defined by two chords of the circle sharing an endpoint.

An _____ is said to intercept an arc on the circle.

a. Inscribed Angle
b. AA postulate
c. ADHM construction
d. ADE classification

22. In geometry, a _____ is a polygon with four 'sides' or edges and four vertices or corners. Sometimes, the term quadrangle is used, for analogy with triangle, and sometimes tetragon for consistency with pentagon (5-sided), hexagon (6-sided) and so on. The word _____ is made of the words quad and lateral.
a. 11-cell
b. -module
c. 1-center problem
d. Quadrilateral

23. In formal mathematical logic, the concept of a _____ may be taken to mean a formula that can be derived according to the derivation rules of a fixed formal system. The statements of a theory as expressed in a formal language are called its elementary _____ s and are said to be true.

The essential property of _____ s is that they are derivable using a fixed set of inference rules and axioms without any additional assumptions.

a. Logical axioms
b. Proof
c. Rule of inference
d. Theorem

24. A _____ is one of the basic shapes of geometry: a polygon with three corners or vertices and three sides or edges which are line segments. A _____ with vertices A, B, and C is denoted ABC.

In Euclidean geometry any three non-collinear points determine a unique _____ and a unique plane (i.e. a two-dimensional Euclidean space.)

   a. -module

   c. 11-cell

   b. 1-center problem

   d. Triangle

Chapter 10. CONSTRUCTIONS AND LOCI

1. A _____, magnetic _____ or mariner's _____ is a navigational instrument for determining direction relative to the earth's magnetic poles. It consists of a magnetized pointer (usually marked on the North end) free to align itself with Earth's magnetic field. The _____ greatly improved the safety and efficiency of travel, especially ocean travel.
    a. 11-cell
    b. -module
    c. 1-center problem
    d. Compass

2. A _____ is a tool with an accurately straight edge used for drawing or cutting straight lines, or checking the straightness of lines. If it has equally spaced markings along its length it is usually called a ruler.

    True straightness can in some cases be checked by using a laser line level as an optical _____: it can illuminate an accurately straight line on a flat surface such as the edge of a plank or shelf.

    a. Feeler gauge
    b. Straightedge
    c. Machinist square
    d. Spirit level

3. In geometry, two sets of points are called _____ if one can be transformed into the other by an isometry, i.e., a combination of translations, rotations and reflections. Less formally, two figures are _____ if they have the same shape and size, but are in different positions (for instance one may be rotated, flipped, or simply placed somewhere else).
    a. Congruent
    b. 1-center problem
    c. -module
    d. 11-cell

4. In geometry and trigonometry, an _____ is the figure formed by two rays sharing a common endpoint, called the vertex of the _____ . The magnitude of the _____ is the 'amount of rotation' that separates the two rays, and can be measured by considering the length of circular arc swept out when one ray is rotated about the vertex to coincide with the other Where there is no possibility of confusion, the term '_____' is used interchangeably for both the geometric configuration itself and for its angular magnitude (which is simply a numerical quantity.)
    a. ADHM construction
    b. ADE classification
    c. AA postulate
    d. Angle

5. In geometry, bisection is the division of something into two equal or congruent parts, usually by a line, which is then called a bisector. The most often considered types of bisectors are segment bisectors and _____. Bisection of a line segment using a compass and ruler Bisection of an angle using a compass and ruler
    a. Angle bisectors
    b. Annulus
    c. Axis of symmetry
    d. Inscribed sphere

6. In geometry, an _____ polygon is a polygon which has all sides of the same length.

    For instance, an _____ triangle is a triangle of equal edge lengths. All _____ triangles are similar to each other, and have 60 degree internal angles.

    a. Octagon
    b. Octadecagon
    c. Enneagram
    d. Equilateral

7. In geometry, an _____ is a triangle in which all three sides are equal. In traditional or Euclidean geometry, _____s are also equiangular; that is, all three internal angles are also congruent to each other and are each 60°. They are regular polygons, and can therefore also be referred to as regular triangles.

a. Orthocenter
b. AA postulate
c. ADE classification
d. Equilateral triangle

8. A _____ is one of the basic shapes of geometry: a polygon with three corners or vertices and three sides or edges which are line segments. A _____ with vertices A, B, and C is denoted ABC.

In Euclidean geometry any three non-collinear points determine a unique _____ and a unique plane (i.e. a two-dimensional Euclidean space.)

a. -module
b. 11-cell
c. 1-center problem
d. Triangle

9. In geometry, two lines or planes (or a line and a plane), are considered _____ to each other if they form congruent adjacent angles (an L-shape.) The term may be used as a noun or adjective. Thus, referring to Figure 1, the line AB is the _____ to CD through the point B. Note that by definition, a line is infinitely long, and strictly speaking AB and CD in this example represent line segments of two infinitely long lines.

a. Perpendicular
b. Heilbronn triangle problem
c. Partial linear space
d. Point group in two dimensions

10. In geometry, bisection is the division of something into two equal or congruent parts, usually by a line, which is then called a bisector. The most often considered types of bisectors are segment bisectors and angle bisectors. Bisection of a line segment using a compass and ruler Bisection of an angle using a compass and ruler Line DE bisects line AB at D, line EF is a _____ of segment AD at C and the interior bisector of right angle AED

A line segment bisector passes through the midpoint of the segment.

a. 1-center problem
b. -module
c. 11-cell
d. Perpendicular bisector

11. In geometry, topology and related branches of mathematics a spatial _____ describes a specific object within a given space that consists of neither volume, area, length, nor any other higher dimensional analogue. Thus, a _____ is a 0-dimensional object. Because of their nature as one of the simplest geometric concepts, they are often used in one form or another as the fundamental constituents of geometry, physics, vector graphics, and many other fields.

a. -module
b. 11-cell
c. 1-center problem
d. Point

12. A _____ of a curve is the envelope of a family of congruent circles centered on the curve. It generalises the concept of _____ lines.

It is sometimes called the offset curve but the term 'offset' often refers also to translation.

a. Trisectrix of Maclaurin
b. Parallel
c. Cissoid
d. Cassini oval

Chapter 10. CONSTRUCTIONS AND LOCI

13. A _____ is a rectangle whose side lengths are in the golden ratio, 1: [x] > (one-to-phi), that is, [x] > or approximately 1:1.618.

A distinctive feature of this shape is that when a square section is removed, the remainder is another _____; that is, with the same proportions as the first. Square removal can be repeated infinitely, in which case corresponding corners of the squares form an infinite sequence of points on the golden spiral, the unique logarithmic spiral with this property.

a. Golden rectangle
b. 11-cell
c. -module
d. 1-center problem

14. In Euclidean geometry, a _____ is a quadrilateral with four right angles. Equivalently, it is an equiangular quadrilateral, but it is not necessarily equilateral.

A _____ with vertices ABCD would be denoted as ABCD.

- All angles are 90 degrees.
- Opposite sides are equal in length.
- Opposite sides are parallel.
- Diagonals are equal in length and bisect each other.

The formula for the perimeter of a _____.

If a _____ has length l and width w

- it has area A = lw
- perimeter P = 2l + 2w = 2(l + w)
- and each diagonal has length $\sqrt{l^2 + w^2}$.

When the length is equal to the width, the _____ is a square.

a. 11-cell
b. 1-center problem
c. -module
d. Rectangle

15. In geometry, three or more lines are said to be concurrent if they intersect at a single point.

In a triangle, four basic types of _____ are altitudes, angle bisectors, medians, and perpendicular bisectors:

- In a triangle, altitudes run from each vertex and meet the opposite side at right-angles. The point where three altitudes meet is the orthocenter.

- Angle bisectors are rays running from the bisector of each angle of the triangle. They all meet at the incenter.

- Medians connect the vertices in a triangle to the midpoint of the opposite side. They meet at the centroid.

a. Concurrent lines
b. 1-center problem
c. Corollary
d. -module

16. A _____ is one of the most curvilinear basic geometric shapes:It has two faces, zero vertices, and zero edges. The surface formed by the points at a fixed distance from a given straight line, the axis of the _____. The solid enclosed by this surface and by two planes perpendicular to the axis is also called a _____.

a. 11-cell
b. 1-center problem
c. -module
d. Cylinder

17. In probability theory and statistics, a _____ is described as the number separating the higher half of a sample, a population from the lower half. The _____ of a finite list of numbers can be found by arranging all the observations from lowest value to highest value and picking the middle one. If there is an even number of observations, the _____ is not unique, so one often takes the mean of the two middle values.

a. 1-center problem
b. Median
c. -module
d. 11-cell

18. In geometry, the circumscribed circle or circumcircle of a polygon is a circle which passes through all the vertices of the polygon. The center of this circle is called the _____.

A polygon which has a circumscribed circle is called a cyclic polygon.

a. Circular sector
b. Circumscribed
c. Circumcenter
d. Nine-Point Circle

19. In geometry, the incircle or inscribed circle of a triangle is the largest circle contained in the triangle; it touches (is tangent to) the three sides. The center of the incircle is called the triangle's _____.

An excircle or escribed circle of the triangle is a circle lying outside the triangle, tangent to one of its sides and tangent to the extensions of the other two.

a. ADE classification
b. Osculating circle
c. AA postulate
d. Incenter

Chapter 10. CONSTRUCTIONS AND LOCI

20. The three altitudes intersect in a single point, called the _____ of the triangle. The _____ lies inside the triangle (and consequently the feet of the altitudes all fall on the triangle) if and only if the triangle is not obtuse (i.e. does not have an angle greater than a right angle.) See also orthocentric system.
    a. ADE classification
    b. Equilateral triangle
    c. Orthocenter
    d. AA postulate

21. An _____ describes the structure and behaviour of applications used in a business, focused on how they interact with each other and with users. It is focused on the data consumed and produced by applications rather than their internal structure. In application portfolio management, the applications are usually mapped to business functions and to application platform technologies.
    a. ADHM construction
    b. Applications architecture
    c. ADE classification
    d. AA postulate

22. The _____ of a system of particles is a specific point at which, for many purposes, the system's mass behaves as if it were concentrated. The _____ is a function only of the positions and masses of the particles that comprise the system. In the case of a rigid body, the position of its _____ is fixed in relation to the object (but not necessarily in contact with it.)
    a. Center of mass
    b. 1-center problem
    c. -module
    d. 11-cell

23. A _____ is a simple shape of Euclidean geometry consisting of those points in a plane which are the same distance from a given point called the centre. The common distance of the points of a _____ from its center is called its radius.

    _____s are simple closed curves which divide the plane into two regions, an interior and an exterior.

    a. -module
    b. Circle
    c. 11-cell
    d. 1-center problem

24. In geometry, the _____ line (or simply the _____) to a curve at a given point is the straight line that 'just touches' the curve at that point (in the sense explained more precisely below.) As it passes through the point of tangency, the _____ line is 'going in the same direction' as the curve, and in this sense it is the best straight-line approximation to the curve at that point. The same definition applies to space curves and curves in n-dimensional Euclidean space.
    a. Tangent
    b. Cartan connection
    c. Metric signature
    d. Measuring function

25. In geometry, the _____ circle or circumcircle of a polygon is a circle which passes through all the vertices of the polygon. The center of this circle is called the circumcenter.

    A polygon which has a _____ circle is called a cyclic polygon.

    a. Circular sector
    b. Circumscribed
    c. Circumcenter
    d. Circle sector

Chapter 10. CONSTRUCTIONS AND LOCI

26. In geometry, an _____ planar shape or solid is one that is enclosed by and 'fits snugly' inside another geometric shape or solid. Specifically, at all points where figures meet, their edges must lie tangent. There must be no object similar to the _____ object but larger and also enclosed by the outer figure.
    a. Octomino
    b. Isometry group
    c. Order-4 dodecahedral honeycomb
    d. Inscribed

27. The problem of _____ is a classic problem of compass and straightedge constructions of ancient Greek mathematics. Two tools are allowed

    1. An un-marked straightedge, and
    2. a compass,

    Problem: construct an angle one-third a given arbitrary angle.

    With such tools, it is generally impossible. This requires taking a cube root, impossible with the given tools.

    a. -module
    b. 1-center problem
    c. 11-cell
    d. Trisecting the angle

28. Angle _____: using only a ruler and a compass, construct an angle that is one-third of a given arbitrary angle. With a straightedge and compass, it is in general impossible. For example, the angle of π/3 radians (60°) cannot be trisected, though, say, 2π/5 radians (72°) may be trisected.
    a. Descartes' theorem
    b. Constructible number
    c. Trisection
    d. Japanese theorem

29. In mathematics, a _____ is a collection of points which share a property. The term _____ is usually used of a condition which defines a continuous figure or figures, that is, a curve. For example, in two-dimensional space a line is the _____ of points equidistant from two fixed points or from two parallel lines.
    a. 9-j symbols
    b. Centered polygonal numbers
    c. Locus
    d. Barycentric coordinates

30. In geometry, the _____ is a circle that can be constructed for any given triangle. It is so named because it passes through nine significant points, six lying on the triangle itself (unless the triangle is obtuse.) They include:

    - The midpoint of each side of the triangle
    - The foot of each altitude
    - The midpoint of the segment of each altitude from its vertex to the orthocenter (where the three altitudes meet)

    The _____ is also known as Feuerbach's circle, Euler's circle, Terquem's circle, the six-points circle, the twelve-points circle, the n-point circle, the medioscribed circle, the mid circle or the circum-midcircle.

    a. Circumcenter
    b. Circle sector
    c. Circular sector
    d. Nine-Point Circle

Chapter 10. CONSTRUCTIONS AND LOCI

31. A timeline of _____ and geometry

- ca. 2000 BC -- Scotland, Carved Stone Balls exhibit a variety of symmetries including all of the symmetries of Platonic solids.
- 1800 BC -- Moscow Mathematical Papyrus, findings volume of a frustum
- 1650 BC -- Rhind Mathematical Papyrus, copy of a lost scroll from around 1850 BC, the scribe Ahmes presents one of the first known approximate values of π at 3.16, the first attempt at squaring the circle, earliest known use of a sort of cotangent, and knowledge of solving first order linear equations
- 1300 BC -- Berlin papyrus (19th dynasty) contains a quadratic equation and its solution.
- 800 BC -- Baudhayana, author of the Baudhayana Sulba Sutra, a Vedic Sanskrit geometric text, contains quadratic equations, and calculates the square root of 2 correct to five decimal places
- ca. 600 BC -- the other Vedic 'Sulba Sutras' use Pythagorean triples, contain of a number of geometrical proofs, and approximate π at 3.16
- 5th century BC -- Hippocrates of Chios utilizes lunes in an attempt to square the circle
- 5th century BC -- Apastamba, author of the Apastamba Sulba Sutra, another Vedic Sanskrit geometric text, makes an attempt at squaring the circle and also calculates the square root of 2 correct to five decimal places
- 530 BC -- Pythagoras studies propositional geometry and vibrating lyre strings; his group also discover the irrationality of the square root of two,
- 370 BC -- Eudoxus states the method of exhaustion for area determination
- 300 BC -- Euclid in his Elements studies geometry as an axiomatic system, proves the infinitude of prime numbers and presents the Euclidean algorithm; he states the law of reflection in Catoptrics, and he proves the fundamental theorem of arithmetic
- 260 BC -- Archimedes proved that the value of π lies between 3 + 1/7 and 3 + 10/71 (approx. 3.1408), that the area of a circle was equal to π multiplied by the square of the radius of the circle and that the area enclosed by a parabola and a straight line is 4/3 multiplied by the area of a triangle with equal base and height. He also gave a very accurate estimate of the value of the square root of 3.
- 225 BC -- Apollonius of Perga writes On Conic Sections and names the ellipse, parabola, and hyperbola,
- 150 BC -- Jain mathematicians in India write the 'Sthananga Sutra', which contains work on the theory of numbers, arithmetical operations, geometry, operations with fractions, simple equations, cubic equations, quartic equations, and permutations and combinations
- 140 BC -- Hipparchus develops the bases of trigonometry.
- 1st century -- Heron of Alexandria, the earliest fleeting reference to square roots of negative numbers.
- 250 -- Diophantus uses symbols for unknown numbers in terms of syncopated _____, and writes Arithmetica, one of the earliest treatises on _____
- ca. 340 -- Pappus of Alexandria states his hexagon theorem and his centroid theorem
- 500 -- Aryabhata writes the 'Aryabhata-Siddhanta', which first introduces the trigonometric functions and methods of calculating their approximate numerical values. It defines the concepts of sine and cosine, and also contains the earliest tables of sine and cosine values
- 600s -- Bhaskara I gives a rational approximation of the sine function
- 600s -- Brahmagupta invents the method of solving indeterminate equations of the second degree and is the first to use _____ to solve astronomical problems. He also develops methods for calculations of the motions and places of various planets, their rising and setting, conjunctions, and the calculation of eclipses of the sun and the moon
- 628 -- Brahmagupta writes the Brahma-sphuta-siddhanta, where zero is clearly explained, and where the modern place-value Indian numeral system is fully developed. It also gives rules for manipulating both negative and positive numbers, methods for computing square roots, methods of solving linear and quadratic equations, and rules for summing series, Brahmagupta's identity, and the Brahmagupta theorem
- 700s -- Virasena gives explicit rules for the Fibonacci sequence, gives the derivation of the volume of a frustum using an infinite procedure, and also deals with the logarithm to base 2 and knows its laws
- 700s -- Shridhara gives the rule for finding the volume of a sphere and also the formula for solving quadratic equations
- 820 -- Al-Khwarizmi -- Persian mathematician, father of _____, writes the Al-Jabr, later transliterated as _____, which introduces systematic algebraic techniques for solving linear and quadratic equations. Translations of his book on arithmetic will introduce the Hindu-Arabic decimal number system to the Western world in the 12th century.

The term algorithm is also named after him.
- 820 -- Al-Mahani conceived the idea of reducing geometrical problems such as doubling the cube to problems in _____.
- 895 -- Thabit ibn Qurra: the only surviving fragment of his original work contains a chapter on the solution and properties of cubic equations. He also generalized the Pythagorean theorem, and discovered the theorem by which pairs of amicable numbers can be found, .
- ca. 900 -- Abu Kamil of Egypt had begun to understand what we would write in symbols as $x^n \cdot x^m = x^{m+n}$
- 953 -- Al-Karaji is the 'first person to completely free _____ from geometrical operations and to replace them with the arithmetical type of operations which are at the core of _____ today. He was first to define the monomials x, x^2, x^3, … and 1 / x, 1 / x^2, 1 / x^3, … and to give rules for products of any two of these. He started a school of _____ which flourished for several hundreds of years'. He also discovered the binomial theorem for integer exponents, which 'was a major factor in the development of numerical analysis based on the decimal system.'
- 975 -- Al-Batani -- Extended the Indian concepts of sine and cosine to other trigonometrical ratios, like tangent, secant and their inverse functions. Derived the formula: $\sin \alpha = \tan \alpha / \sqrt{1 + \tan^2 \alpha}$ and $\cos \alpha = 1 / \sqrt{1 + \tan^2 \alpha}$.
- ca. 1000 -- Abū Sahl al-Qūhī (Kuhi) solves equations higher than the second degree.
- ca. 1000 -- Law of sines is discovered by Muslim mathematicians, but it is uncertain who discovers it first between Abu-Mahmud al-Khujandi, Abu Nasr Mansur, and Abu al-Wafa.
- 1070 -- Omar Khayyám begins to write Treatise on Demonstration of Problems of _____ and classifies cubic equations.
- ca. 1100 -- Omar Khayyám 'gave a complete classification of cubic equations with geometric solutions found by means of intersecting conic sections.' He became the first to find general geometric solutions of cubic equations and laid the foundations for the development of analytic geometry and non-Euclidean geometry. He also extracted roots using the decimal system .
- 1100s -- Bhaskara Acharya writes the 'Bijaganita' , which is the first text that recognizes that a positive number has two square roots
- 1130 -- Al-Samawal gave a definition of _____: '[it is concerned] with operating on unknowns using all the arithmetical tools, in the same way as the arithmetician operates on the known.'
- 1135 -- Sharafeddin Tusi followed al-Khayyam's application of _____ to geometry, and wrote a treatise on cubic equations which 'represents an essential contribution to another _____ which aimed to study curves by means of equations, thus inaugurating the beginning of algebraic geometry.'
- ca. 1250 -- Nasir Al-Din Al-Tusi attempts to develop a form of non-Euclidean geometry.
- 1400s -- Nilakantha Somayaji, a Kerala school mathematician, writes the 'Aryabhatiya Bhasya', which contains work on infinite-series expansions, problems of _____, and spherical geometry

- 1520 -- Scipione dal Ferro develops a method for solving 'depressed' cubic equations (cubic equations without an x^2 term), but does not publish.
- 1535 -- Niccolo Tartaglia independently develops a method for solving depressed cubic equations but also does not publish.
- 1539 -- Gerolamo Cardano learns Tartaglia's method for solving depressed cubics and discovers a method for depressing cubics, thereby creating a method for solving all cubics.
- 1540 -- Lodovico Ferrari solves the quartic equation.

- 1600s - Putumana Somayaji writes the 'Paddhati', which presents a detailed discussion of various trigonometric series
- 1619 - René Descartes discovers analytic geometry (Pierre de Fermat claimed that he also discovered it independently),
- 1619 - Johannes Kepler discovers two of the Kepler-Poinsot polyhedra.
- 1637 - Pierre de Fermat claims to have proven Fermat's Last Theorem in his copy of Diophantus' Arithmetica,
- 1637 - First use of the term imaginary number by René Descartes; it was meant to be derogatory.

- 1722 - Abraham de Moivre states de Moivre's formula connecting trigonometric functions and complex numbers,
- 1733 - Giovanni Gerolamo Saccheri studies what geometry would be like if Euclid's fifth postulate were false,
- 1796 - Carl Friedrich Gauss proves that the regular 17-gon can be constructed using only a compass and straightedge
- 1797 - Caspar Wessel associates vectors with complex numbers and studies complex number operations in geometrical terms,
- 1799 - Carl Friedrich Gauss proves the fundamental theorem of _____,

- 1799 - Paolo Ruffini partially proves the Abel-Ruffini theorem that quintic or higher equations cannot be solved by a general formula,

- 1806 - Louis Poinsot discovers the two remaining Kepler-Poinsot polyhedra.
- 1806 - Jean-Robert Argand publishes proof of the Fundamental theorem of _____ and the Argand diagram,
- 1824 - Niels Henrik Abel partially proves the Abel-Ruffini theorem that the general quintic or higher equations cannot be solved by a general formula involving only arithmetical operations and roots,
- 1829 - Bolyai, Gauss, and Lobachevsky invent hyperbolic non-Euclidean geometry,
- 1832 - Évariste Galois presents a general condition for the solvability of algebraic equations, thereby essentially founding group theory and Galois theory,
- 1837 - Pierre Wantsel proves that doubling the cube and trisecting the angle are impossible with only a compass and straightedge, as well as the full completion of the problem of constructability of regular polygons
- 1843 - William Hamilton discovers the calculus of quaternions and deduces that they are non-commutative,
- 1847 - George Boole formalizes symbolic logic in The Mathematical Analysis of Logic, defining what now is called Boolean _____,
- 1854 - Bernhard Riemann introduces Riemannian geometry,
- 1854 - Arthur Cayley shows that quaternions can be used to represent rotations in four-dimensional space,
- 1858 - August Ferdinand Möbius invents the Möbius strip,
- 1870 - Felix Klein constructs an analytic geometry for Lobachevski's geometry thereby establishing its self-consistency and the logical independence of Euclid's fifth postulate,
- 1873 - Charles Hermite proves that e is transcendental,
- 1878 - Charles Hermite solves the general quintic equation by means of elliptic and modular functions
- 1882 - Ferdinand von Lindemann proves that π is transcendental and that therefore the circle cannot be squared with a compass and straightedge,
- 1882 - Felix Klein invents the Klein bottle,
- 1899 - David Hilbert presents a set of self-consistent geometric axioms in Foundations of Geometry,

- 1901 - Élie Cartan develops the exterior derivative,
- 1905 - Einstein's theory of special relativity.
- 1912 - Luitzen Egbertus Jan Brouwer presents the Brouwer fixed-point theorem,
- 1916 - Einstein's theory of general relativity.
- 1930 - Casimir Kuratowski shows that the three-cottage problem has no solution,
- 1931 - Georges de Rham develops theorems in cohomology and characteristic classes,
- 1933 - Karol Borsuk and Stanislaw Ulam present the Borsuk-Ulam antipodal-point theorem,
- 1955 - H. S. M. Coxeter et al. publish the complete list of uniform polyhedron,
- 1981 - Mikhail Gromov develops the theory of hyperbolic groups, revolutionizing both infinite group theory and global differential geometry,
- 1983 - the classification of finite simple groups, a collaborative work involving some hundred mathematicians and spanning thirty years, is completed,
- 1991 - Alain Connes and John W. Lott develop non-commutative geometry,
- 1998 - Thomas Callister Hales (almost certainly) proves the Kepler conjecture,

- 2003 - Grigori Perelman proves the Poincaré conjecture,
- 2007 - a team of researches throughout North America and Europe used networks of computers to map E8 (mathematics.)

Chapter 10. CONSTRUCTIONS AND LOCI

    a. ADHM construction   b. ADE classification
    c. AA postulate   d. Algebra

32. In each statement above, a is not equal to b. These relations are known as strict _____. The notation a < b may also be read as 'a is strictly less than b'.
    a. ADE classification   b. ADHM construction
    c. AA postulate   d. Inequalities

33. In chemistry, the _____ molecular geometry describes the arrangement of three or more atoms placed at an expected bond angle of 180°. _____ organic molecules, e.g. acetylene, are often described by invoking sp orbital hybridization for the carbon centers. Many _____ molecules exist, prominent examples include CO_2, HCN, and xenon difluoride.
    a. 11-cell   b. -module
    c. 1-center problem   d. Linear

34. where a is any scalar. A function which satisfies these properties is called a linear function, or more generally a linear map. This property makes _____ s particularly easy to solve and reason about.
    a. -module   b. 11-cell
    c. 1-center problem   d. Linear equation

35. In mathematics, the _____ of a real number is its numerical value without regard to its sign. So, for example, 3 is the _____ of both 3 and −3.

The _____ of a number a is denoted by | a |.

    a. ADE classification   b. ADHM construction
    c. AA postulate   d. Absolute value

Chapter 11. AREAS OF PLANE FIGURES

1. In Euclidean geometry, a _____ is a regular quadrilateral. This means that it has four equal sides and four equal angles (90 degree angles, or right angles.) A _____ with vertices ABCD would be denoted ABCD.
   - a. 11-cell
   - b. Square
   - c. -module
   - d. 1-center problem

2. In geometry, two sets of points are called _____ if one can be transformed into the other by an isometry, i.e., a combination of translations, rotations and reflections. Less formally, two figures are _____ if they have the same shape and size, but are in different positions (for instance one may be rotated, flipped, or simply placed somewhere else).
   - a. 11-cell
   - b. -module
   - c. 1-center problem
   - d. Congruent

3. In geometry, a _____ is a quadrilateral with two sets of parallel sides. The opposite or facing sides of a _____ are of equal length, and the opposite angles of a _____ are of equal size. The three-dimensional counterpart of a _____ is a parallelepiped.
   - a. -module
   - b. 11-cell
   - c. Parallelogram
   - d. 1-center problem

4. In Euclidean geometry, a _____ is a quadrilateral with four right angles. Equivalently, it is an equiangular quadrilateral, but it is not necessarily equilateral.

A _____ with vertices ABCD would be denoted as ABCD.

- All angles are 90 degrees.
- Opposite sides are equal in length.
- Opposite sides are parallel.
- Diagonals are equal in length and bisect each other.

The formula for the perimeter of a _____.

If a _____ has length l and width w

- it has area A = lw
- perimeter P = 2l + 2w = 2(l + w)
- and each diagonal has length $\sqrt{l^2 + w^2}$.

When the length is equal to the width, the _____ is a square.

   - a. 11-cell
   - b. Rectangle
   - c. 1-center problem
   - d. -module

5. In linear algebra, a (linear) _____ is a subset of a vector space that is closed under multiplication by positive scalars. In other words, a subset C of a real vector space V is a _____ if and only if >λx belongs to C for any x in C and any positive scalar >λ of V (or, more succintly, if and only if >λC = C for any positive scalar >λ.)

A _____ is said to be pointed if it includes the null vector (origin) 0; otherwise it is said to be blunt.

Chapter 11. AREAS OF PLANE FIGURES

a. Cone
b. Centerpoint
c. Prismatic surface
d. Complex line

6. A _____ is one of the most curvilinear basic geometric shapes: It has two faces, zero vertices, and zero edges. The surface formed by the points at a fixed distance from a given straight line, the axis of the _____. The solid enclosed by this surface and by two planes perpendicular to the axis is also called a _____.
   a. 11-cell
   b. -module
   c. 1-center problem
   d. Cylinder

7. An _____ describes the structure and behaviour of applications used in a business, focused on how they interact with each other and with users. It is focused on the data consumed and produced by applications rather than their internal structure. In application portfolio management, the applications are usually mapped to business functions and to application platform technologies.
   a. ADE classification
   b. ADHM construction
   c. AA postulate
   d. Applications architecture

8. In a totally ordered set all elements are mutually comparable, so such a set can have at most one minimal element and at most one maximal element. Then, due to mutual comparability, the minimal element will also be the least element and the maximal element will also be the greatest element. Thus in a totally ordered set we can simply use the terms minimum and _____.
   a. Fresnel integrals
   b. Hyperbolic angle
   c. -module
   d. Maximum

9. Integration is an important concept in mathematics which, together with differentiation, forms one of the main operations in calculus. Given a function $>f$ of a real variable x and an interval [a, b] of the real line, the _____

is defined informally to be the net signed area of the region in the xy-plane bounded by the graph of $>f$, the x-axis, and the vertical lines x = a and x = b.

The term integral may also refer to the notion of antiderivative, a function F whose derivative is the given function $>f$.

   a. 11-cell
   b. -module
   c. 1-center problem
   d. Definite integral

10. In mathematics, a _____ consists of the points through which a continuously moving point passes. This notion captures the intuitive idea of a geometrical one-dimensional object, which furthermore is connected in the sense of having no discontinuities or gaps. Simple examples include the sine wave as the basic _____ underlying simple harmonic motion, and the parabola.
    a. Sectrix of Maclaurin
    b. Dual curve
    c. Singular point
    d. Curve

Chapter 11. AREAS OF PLANE FIGURES

11. A _____ is one of the basic shapes of geometry: a polygon with three corners or vertices and three sides or edges which are line segments. A _____ with vertices A, B, and C is denoted ABC.

In Euclidean geometry any three non-collinear points determine a unique _____ and a unique plane (i.e. a two-dimensional Euclidean space.)

a. 1-center problem
c. -module

b. Triangle
d. 11-cell

Chapter 11. AREAS OF PLANE FIGURES

12. A timeline of _____ and geometry

- ca. 2000 BC -- Scotland, Carved Stone Balls exhibit a variety of symmetries including all of the symmetries of Platonic solids.
- 1800 BC -- Moscow Mathematical Papyrus, findings volume of a frustum
- 1650 BC -- Rhind Mathematical Papyrus, copy of a lost scroll from around 1850 BC, the scribe Ahmes presents one of the first known approximate values of π at 3.16, the first attempt at squaring the circle, earliest known use of a sort of cotangent, and knowledge of solving first order linear equations
- 1300 BC -- Berlin papyrus (19th dynasty) contains a quadratic equation and its solution.

- 800 BC -- Baudhayana, author of the Baudhayana Sulba Sutra, a Vedic Sanskrit geometric text, contains quadratic equations, and calculates the square root of 2 correct to five decimal places
- ca. 600 BC -- the other Vedic 'Sulba Sutras' use Pythagorean triples, contain of a number of geometrical proofs, and approximate π at 3.16
- 5th century BC -- Hippocrates of Chios utilizes lunes in an attempt to square the circle
- 5th century BC -- Apastamba, author of the Apastamba Sulba Sutra, another Vedic Sanskrit geometric text, makes an attempt at squaring the circle and also calculates the square root of 2 correct to five decimal places
- 530 BC -- Pythagoras studies propositional geometry and vibrating lyre strings; his group also discover the irrationality of the square root of two,
- 370 BC -- Eudoxus states the method of exhaustion for area determination
- 300 BC -- Euclid in his Elements studies geometry as an axiomatic system, proves the infinitude of prime numbers and presents the Euclidean algorithm; he states the law of reflection in Catoptrics, and he proves the fundamental theorem of arithmetic
- 260 BC -- Archimedes proved that the value of π lies between 3 + 1/7 and 3 + 10/71 (approx. 3.1408), that the area of a circle was equal to π multiplied by the square of the radius of the circle and that the area enclosed by a parabola and a straight line is 4/3 multiplied by the area of a triangle with equal base and height. He also gave a very accurate estimate of the value of the square root of 3.
- 225 BC -- Apollonius of Perga writes On Conic Sections and names the ellipse, parabola, and hyperbola,
- 150 BC -- Jain mathematicians in India write the 'Sthananga Sutra', which contains work on the theory of numbers, arithmetical operations, geometry, operations with fractions, simple equations, cubic equations, quartic equations, and permutations and combinations
- 140 BC -- Hipparchus develops the bases of trigonometry.

- 1st century -- Heron of Alexandria, the earliest fleeting reference to square roots of negative numbers.
- 250 -- Diophantus uses symbols for unknown numbers in terms of syncopated _____, and writes Arithmetica, one of the earliest treatises on _____
- ca. 340 -- Pappus of Alexandria states his hexagon theorem and his centroid theorem
- 500 -- Aryabhata writes the 'Aryabhata-Siddhanta', which first introduces the trigonometric functions and methods of calculating their approximate numerical values. It defines the concepts of sine and cosine, and also contains the earliest tables of sine and cosine values
- 600s -- Bhaskara I gives a rational approximation of the sine function
- 600s -- Brahmagupta invents the method of solving indeterminate equations of the second degree and is the first to use _____ to solve astronomical problems. He also develops methods for calculations of the motions and places of various planets, their rising and setting, conjunctions, and the calculation of eclipses of the sun and the moon
- 628 -- Brahmagupta writes the Brahma-sphuta-siddhanta, where zero is clearly explained, and where the modern place-value Indian numeral system is fully developed. It also gives rules for manipulating both negative and positive numbers, methods for computing square roots, methods of solving linear and quadratic equations, and rules for summing series, Brahmagupta's identity, and the Brahmagupta theorem
- 700s -- Virasena gives explicit rules for the Fibonacci sequence, gives the derivation of the volume of a frustum using an infinite procedure, and also deals with the logarithm to base 2 and knows its laws
- 700s -- Shridhara gives the rule for finding the volume of a sphere and also the formula for solving quadratic equations
- 820 -- Al-Khwarizmi -- Persian mathematician, father of _____, writes the Al-Jabr, later transliterated as _____, which introduces systematic algebraic techniques for solving linear and quadratic equations. Translations of his book on arithmetic will introduce the Hindu-Arabic decimal number system to the Western world in the 12th century.

The term algorithm is also named after him.
- 820 -- Al-Mahani conceived the idea of reducing geometrical problems such as doubling the cube to problems in _____.
- 895 -- Thabit ibn Qurra: the only surviving fragment of his original work contains a chapter on the solution and properties of cubic equations. He also generalized the Pythagorean theorem, and discovered the theorem by which pairs of amicable numbers can be found, .
- ca. 900 -- Abu Kamil of Egypt had begun to understand what we would write in symbols as $x^n \cdot x^m = x^{m+n}$
- 953 -- Al-Karaji is the 'first person to completely free _____ from geometrical operations and to replace them with the arithmetical type of operations which are at the core of _____ today. He was first to define the monomials x, x^2, x^3, … and 1 / x, 1 / x^2, 1 / x^3, … and to give rules for products of any two of these. He started a school of _____ which flourished for several hundreds of years'. He also discovered the binomial theorem for integer exponents, which 'was a major factor in the development of numerical analysis based on the decimal system.'
- 975 -- Al-Batani -- Extended the Indian concepts of sine and cosine to other trigonometrical ratios, like tangent, secant and their inverse functions. Derived the formula: $\sin\alpha = \tan\alpha / \sqrt{1 + \tan^2\alpha}$ and $\cos\alpha = 1/\sqrt{1 + \tan^2\alpha}$.

- ca. 1000 -- Abū Sahl al-Qūhī (Kuhi) solves equations higher than the second degree.
- ca. 1000 -- Law of sines is discovered by Muslim mathematicians, but it is uncertain who discovers it first between Abu-Mahmud al-Khujandi, Abu Nasr Mansur, and Abu al-Wafa.
- 1070 -- Omar Khayyám begins to write Treatise on Demonstration of Problems of _____ and classifies cubic equations.
- ca. 1100 -- Omar Khayyám 'gave a complete classification of cubic equations with geometric solutions found by means of intersecting conic sections.' He became the first to find general geometric solutions of cubic equations and laid the foundations for the development of analytic geometry and non-Euclidean geometry. He also extracted roots using the decimal system .
- 1100s -- Bhaskara Acharya writes the 'Bijaganita' , which is the first text that recognizes that a positive number has two square roots
- 1130 -- Al-Samawal gave a definition of _____: '[it is concerned] with operating on unknowns using all the arithmetical tools, in the same way as the arithmetician operates on the known.'
- 1135 -- Sharafeddin Tusi followed al-Khayyam's application of _____ to geometry, and wrote a treatise on cubic equations which 'represents an essential contribution to another _____ which aimed to study curves by means of equations, thus inaugurating the beginning of algebraic geometry.'
- ca. 1250 -- Nasir Al-Din Al-Tusi attempts to develop a form of non-Euclidean geometry.
- 1400s -- Nilakantha Somayaji, a Kerala school mathematician, writes the 'Aryabhatiya Bhasya', which contains work on infinite-series expansions, problems of _____, and spherical geometry

- 1520 -- Scipione dal Ferro develops a method for solving 'depressed' cubic equations (cubic equations without an x^2 term), but does not publish.
- 1535 -- Niccolo Tartaglia independently develops a method for solving depressed cubic equations but also does not publish.
- 1539 -- Gerolamo Cardano learns Tartaglia's method for solving depressed cubics and discovers a method for depressing cubics, thereby creating a method for solving all cubics.
- 1540 -- Lodovico Ferrari solves the quartic equation.

- 1600s - Putumana Somayaji writes the 'Paddhati', which presents a detailed discussion of various trigonometric series
- 1619 - René Descartes discovers analytic geometry (Pierre de Fermat claimed that he also discovered it independently),
- 1619 - Johannes Kepler discovers two of the Kepler-Poinsot polyhedra.
- 1637 - Pierre de Fermat claims to have proven Fermat's Last Theorem in his copy of Diophantus' Arithmetica,
- 1637 - First use of the term imaginary number by René Descartes; it was meant to be derogatory.

- 1722 - Abraham de Moivre states de Moivre's formula connecting trigonometric functions and complex numbers,
- 1733 - Giovanni Gerolamo Saccheri studies what geometry would be like if Euclid's fifth postulate were false,
- 1796 - Carl Friedrich Gauss proves that the regular 17-gon can be constructed using only a compass and straightedge
- 1797 - Caspar Wessel associates vectors with complex numbers and studies complex number operations in geometrical terms,
- 1799 - Carl Friedrich Gauss proves the fundamental theorem of _____,

- 1799 - Paolo Ruffini partially proves the Abel-Ruffini theorem that quintic or higher equations cannot be solved by a general formula,

- 1806 - Louis Poinsot discovers the two remaining Kepler-Poinsot polyhedra.
- 1806 - Jean-Robert Argand publishes proof of the Fundamental theorem of _____ and the Argand diagram,
- 1824 - Niels Henrik Abel partially proves the Abel-Ruffini theorem that the general quintic or higher equations cannot be solved by a general formula involving only arithmetical operations and roots,
- 1829 - Bolyai, Gauss, and Lobachevsky invent hyperbolic non-Euclidean geometry,
- 1832 - Évariste Galois presents a general condition for the solvability of algebraic equations, thereby essentially founding group theory and Galois theory,
- 1837 - Pierre Wantsel proves that doubling the cube and trisecting the angle are impossible with only a compass and straightedge, as well as the full completion of the problem of constructability of regular polygons
- 1843 - William Hamilton discovers the calculus of quaternions and deduces that they are non-commutative,
- 1847 - George Boole formalizes symbolic logic in The Mathematical Analysis of Logic, defining what now is called Boolean _____,
- 1854 - Bernhard Riemann introduces Riemannian geometry,
- 1854 - Arthur Cayley shows that quaternions can be used to represent rotations in four-dimensional space,
- 1858 - August Ferdinand Möbius invents the Möbius strip,
- 1870 - Felix Klein constructs an analytic geometry for Lobachevski's geometry thereby establishing its self-consistency and the logical independence of Euclid's fifth postulate,
- 1873 - Charles Hermite proves that e is transcendental,
- 1878 - Charles Hermite solves the general quintic equation by means of elliptic and modular functions
- 1882 - Ferdinand von Lindemann proves that π is transcendental and that therefore the circle cannot be squared with a compass and straightedge,
- 1882 - Felix Klein invents the Klein bottle,
- 1899 - David Hilbert presents a set of self-consistent geometric axioms in Foundations of Geometry,

- 1901 - Élie Cartan develops the exterior derivative,
- 1905 - Einstein's theory of special relativity.
- 1912 - Luitzen Egbertus Jan Brouwer presents the Brouwer fixed-point theorem,
- 1916 - Einstein's theory of general relativity.
- 1930 - Casimir Kuratowski shows that the three-cottage problem has no solution,
- 1931 - Georges de Rham develops theorems in cohomology and characteristic classes,
- 1933 - Karol Borsuk and Stanislaw Ulam present the Borsuk-Ulam antipodal-point theorem,
- 1955 - H. S. M. Coxeter et al. publish the complete list of uniform polyhedron,
- 1981 - Mikhail Gromov develops the theory of hyperbolic groups, revolutionizing both infinite group theory and global differential geometry,
- 1983 - the classification of finite simple groups, a collaborative work involving some hundred mathematicians and spanning thirty years, is completed,
- 1991 - Alain Connes and John W. Lott develop non-commutative geometry,
- 1998 - Thomas Callister Hales (almost certainly) proves the Kepler conjecture,

- 2003 - Grigori Perelman proves the Poincaré conjecture,
- 2007 - a team of researches throughout North America and Europe used networks of computers to map E8 (mathematics.)

Chapter 11. AREAS OF PLANE FIGURES

a. ADE classification
c. ADHM construction
b. AA postulate
d. Algebra

13.

Every _____ has two diagonals connecting opposite pairs of vertices. Using congruent triangles, one can prove that the _____ is symmetric across each of these diagonals. It follows that any _____ has the following two properties:

1. Opposite angles of a _____ have equal measure.
2. The two diagonals of a _____ are perpendicular.

a. 1-center problem
c. -module
b. 11-cell
d. Rhombus

14. In geometry, a figure with one pair of parallel sides is referred to as _____ in American English, and as a trapezium in British English. A _____ with vertices ABCD is denoted ABCD.

In North America, the term trapezium is used to refer to a quadrilateral with no parallel sides.

a. -module
c. Trapezoid
b. Rhomboid
d. Tangential quadrilateral

15. In mathematics, the _____ or Pythagoras' theorem is a relation in Euclidean geometry among the three sides of a right triangle. The theorem is usually written as an equation:

$$a^2 + b^2 = c^2$$

where c represents the length of the hypotenuse, and a and b represent the lengths of the other two sides. In words:

The square of the hypotenuse of a right triangle is equal to the sum of the squares on the other two sides.

a. 1-center problem
c. -module
b. 11-cell
d. Pythagorean Theorem

16. In formal mathematical logic, the concept of a _____ may be taken to mean a formula that can be derived according to the derivation rules of a fixed formal system. The statements of a theory as expressed in a formal language are called its elementary _____s and are said to be true.

The essential property of _____s is that they are derivable using a fixed set of inference rules and axioms without any additional assumptions.

Chapter 11. AREAS OF PLANE FIGURES

    a. Rule of inference
    b. Logical axioms
    c. Proof
    d. Theorem

17. A _____ is a polygon which is equiangular (all angles are equal in measure) and equilateral (all sides have the same length.) _____s may be convex or star.

These properties apply to both convex and a star _____s.

    a. Regular polygon
    b. Reuleaux triangle
    c. Constructible polygon
    d. Hendecagon

18. In geometry, an _____ planar shape or solid is one that is enclosed by and 'fits snugly' inside another geometric shape or solid. Specifically, at all points where figures meet, their edges must lie tangent. There must be no object similar to the _____ object but larger and also enclosed by the outer figure.

    a. Octomino
    b. Order-4 dodecahedral honeycomb
    c. Isometry group
    d. Inscribed

19. In geometry a _____ is traditionally a plane figure that is bounded by a closed path or circuit, composed of a finite sequence of straight line segments (i.e., by a closed polygonal chain.) These segments are called its edges or sides, and the points where two edges meet are the _____'s vertices or corners. The interior of the _____ is sometimes called its body.

    a. Hexagram
    b. Right triangle
    c. Dodecagon
    d. Polygon

20. In geometry and trigonometry, an _____ is the figure formed by two rays sharing a common endpoint, called the vertex of the _____ . The magnitude of the _____ is the 'amount of rotation' that separates the two rays, and can be measured by considering the length of circular arc swept out when one ray is rotated about the vertex to coincide with the other Where there is no possibility of confusion, the term '_____' is used interchangeably for both the geometric configuration itself and for its angular magnitude (which is simply a numerical quantity.)

    a. AA postulate
    b. Angle
    c. ADHM construction
    d. ADE classification

21. The _____ of a regular polygon is a line segment from the center to the midpoint of one of its sides. Equivalently, it is the line drawn from the center of the polygon that is perpendicular to one of its sides. The word '_____' can also refer to the length of that line segment.

    a. Affine geometry
    b. Equidimensional
    c. Orthogonal trajectories
    d. Apothem

22. A _____ is an angle whose vertex is the center of a circle, and whose sides pass through a pair of points on the circle, thereby subtending an arc between those two points whose angle is (by definition) equal to the _____ itself. It is also known as the arc segment's angular distance.

On a sphere or ellipsoid, the _____ is delineated along a great circle.

Chapter 11. AREAS OF PLANE FIGURES

    a. Central angle
    c. Cuboid
    b. Skew lines
    d. Spidron

23. A _____ is a simple shape of Euclidean geometry consisting of those points in a plane which are the same distance from a given point called the centre. The common distance of the points of a _____ from its center is called its radius.

_____s are simple closed curves which divide the plane into two regions, an interior and an exterior.

    a. Circle
    c. 11-cell
    b. -module
    d. 1-center problem

24. A _____ is a path that surrounds an area. The word comes from the Greek peri and meter (measure.) The term may be used either for the path or its length.

    a. Perimeter
    c. Transversal line
    b. Multilateration
    d. Complementary angles

25. In each statement above, a is not equal to b. These relations are known as strict _____. The notation a < b may also be read as 'a is strictly less than b'.

    a. AA postulate
    c. ADHM construction
    b. ADE classification
    d. Inequalities

26. In chemistry, the _____ molecular geometry describes the arrangement of three or more atoms placed at an expected bond angle of 180Â°. _____ organic molecules, e.g. acetylene, are often described by invoking sp orbital hybridization for the carbon centers. Many _____ molecules exist, prominent examples include CO_2, HCN, and xenon difluoride.

    a. 11-cell
    c. -module
    b. Linear
    d. 1-center problem

27. where a is any scalar. A function which satisfies these properties is called a linear function, or more generally a linear map. This property makes _____s particularly easy to solve and reason about.

    a. 1-center problem
    c. -module
    b. Linear equation
    d. 11-cell

28. In mathematics, the _____ of a real number is its numerical value without regard to its sign. So, for example, 3 is the _____ of both 3 and −3.

The _____ of a number a is denoted by | a | .

    a. ADHM construction
    c. AA postulate
    b. ADE classification
    d. Absolute value

29. A circular sector or _____, is the portion of a circle enclosed by two radii and an arc, where the smaller area is known as the minor sector and the larger being the major sector.

Chapter 11. AREAS OF PLANE FIGURES

a. Circumscribed
c. Circle sector
b. Circular sector
d. Circumcenter

30. Determining the _____ segment--also called rectification of a curve--was historically difficult. Although many methods were used for specific curves, the advent of calculus led to a general formula that provides closed-form solutions in some cases.
   a. -module
   c. 11-cell
   b. 1-center problem
   d. Length of an irregular arc

31. A _____ is a circular chart divided into sectors, illustrating relative magnitudes or frequencies. In a _____, the arc length of each sector (and consequently its central angle and area), is proportional to the quantity it represents. Together, the sectors create a full disk.
   a. Pie chart
   c. -module
   b. 11-cell
   d. 1-center problem

32. A _____ or circle sector, is the portion of a circle enclosed by two radii and an arc, where the smaller area is known as the minor sector and the larger being the major sector. Its area can be calculated as described below.
   a. Nine-Point Circle
   c. Circumcenter
   b. Circle sector
   d. Circular sector

33. In geometry, an _____ is a closed segment of a differentiable curve in the two-dimensional plane; for example, a circular _____ is a segment of the circumference of a circle. If the _____ segment occupies a great circle (or great ellipse), it is considered a great-_____ segment.

The length of an _____ of a circle with radius r and subtending an angle ☐> (measured in radians) with the circle center -- i.e., the central angle -- equals ☐>.

   a. Equiangular polygon
   c. Order-4 dodecahedral honeycomb
   b. Almost symplectic manifold
   d. Arc

34. A _____ is an expression which compares quantities relative to each other. The most common examples involve two quantities, but in theory any number of quantities can be compared. In mathematical terms, they are represented by separating each quantity with a colon, for example the _____ 2:3, which is read as the _____ 'two to three'.
   a. Slope
   c. -module
   b. Slope of a line
   d. Ratio

35. A _____ is a number which scales or multiplies with a quantity.

example the _____ for:

a cookie that was only 1 pound got enlarged to a cookie that is 2 pounds therefore the _____ is 2 because you multiplied the 1 pound by 2 to get the 2 pounds.

Chapter 11. AREAS OF PLANE FIGURES

a. Line field
c. Tarry point
b. Moduli scheme
d. Scale factor

36. One of the meanings of the terms _____ and _____ transformation (also called dilation) of a Euclidean space is a function f from the space into itself that multiplies all distances by the same positive scalar r, so that for any two points x and y we have

$$d(f(x), f(y)) = rd(x,y),$$

where 'd(x,y)' is the Euclidean distance from x to y. Two sets are called similar if one is the image of the other under such a _____.

A special case is a homothetic transformation or central _____: it neither involves rotation nor taking the mirror image.

a. Similar
c. Flat
b. Similarity
d. Square lattice

37. Two geometrical objects are called _____ if they both have the same shape. Equivalently and more precisely, one is congruent to the result of a uniform scaling (enlarging or shrinking) of the other. Corresponding sides of _____ polygons are in proportion, and corresponding angles of _____ polygons have the same measure.
a. Simple polytope
c. Similar
b. Plane
d. Steiner-Lehmus theorem

38. The _____ of any solid, liquid, plasma, vacuum or theoretical object is how much three-dimensional space it occupies, often quantified numerically. One-dimensional figures (such as lines) and two-dimensional shapes (such as squares) are assigned zero _____ in the three-dimensional space. _____ is commonly presented in units such as mL or cm^3 (milliliters or cubic centimeters.)
a. Volume
c. Fractional quantum mechanics
b. Spin
d. Geodesic

Chapter 12. AREAS AND VOLUMES OF SOLIDS

1. In geometry, an n-sided _____ is a polyhedron made of an n-sided polygonal base, a translated copy, and n faces joining corresponding sides. Thus these joining faces are parallelograms. All cross-sections parallel to the base faces are the same.
   - a. Hoberman sphere
   - b. Prism
   - c. Hill tetrahedron
   - d. Defect

2. In linear algebra, a (linear) _____ is a subset of a vector space that is closed under multiplication by positive scalars. In other words, a subset C of a real vector space V is a _____ if and only if >λx belongs to C for any x in C and any positive scalar >λ of V (or, more succintly, if and only if >λC = C for any positive scalar >λ.)

   A _____ is said to be pointed if it includes the null vector (origin) 0; otherwise it is said to be blunt.
   - a. Centerpoint
   - b. Prismatic surface
   - c. Complex line
   - d. Cone

3. A _____ is one of the most curvilinear basic geometric shapes:It has two faces, zero vertices, and zero edges. The surface formed by the points at a fixed distance from a given straight line, the axis of the _____. The solid enclosed by this surface and by two planes perpendicular to the axis is also called a _____.
   - a. -module
   - b. Cylinder
   - c. 11-cell
   - d. 1-center problem

4. A right prism is a prism in which the joining edges and faces are perpendicular to the base faces. This applies if the joining faces are rectangular. If the joining edges and faces are not perpendicular to the base faces, it is called an _____.
   - a. Isohedral
   - b. Omnitruncation
   - c. Uniform polyhedron
   - d. Oblique Prism

5. The _____ of any solid, liquid, plasma, vacuum or theoretical object is how much three-dimensional space it occupies, often quantified numerically. One-dimensional figures (such as lines) and two-dimensional shapes (such as squares) are assigned zero _____ in the three-dimensional space. _____ is commonly presented in units such as mL or cm^3 (milliliters or cubic centimeters.)
   - a. Spin
   - b. Fractional quantum mechanics
   - c. Volume
   - d. Geodesic

6. In technical applications of 3D computer graphics (CAx) such as computer-aided design and computer-aided manufacturing, _____s are one way of representing objects. The other ways are wireframe (lines and curves) and solids. Point clouds are also sometimes used as temporary ways to represent an object, with the goal of using the points to create one or more of the three permanent representations.
   - a. Geometric primitive
   - b. Solid modeling
   - c. Surface
   - d. Space partitioning

7. Area is a quantity expressing the two-dimensional size of a defined part of a surface, typically a region bounded by a closed curve. The term _____ refers to the total area of the exposed surface of a 3-dimensional solid, such as the sum of the areas of the exposed sides of a polyhedron. Area is an important invariant in the differential geometry of surfaces.
   - a. 11-cell
   - b. -module
   - c. 1-center problem
   - d. Surface Area

Chapter 12. AREAS AND VOLUMES OF SOLIDS

8. In a totally ordered set all elements are mutually comparable, so such a set can have at most one minimal element and at most one maximal element. Then, due to mutual comparability, the minimal element will also be the least element and the maximal element will also be the greatest element. Thus in a totally ordered set we can simply use the terms minimum and _____.
    a. Hyperbolic angle
    b. -module
    c. Fresnel integrals
    d. Maximum

9. A _____ is a building where the outer surfaces are triangular and converge at a point. The base of a _____ is usually trilateral or quadrilateral (but may be of any polygon shape), meaning that a _____ usually has four or five faces. A _____'s design, with the majority of the weight closer to the ground, means that less material higher up on the _____ will be pushing down from above: this allowed early civilizations to create stable monumental structures.
    a. 11-cell
    b. -module
    c. 1-center problem
    d. Pyramid

10. In the geometry of curves a _____ is a point of where the first derivative of curvature is zero. This is typically a local maximum or minimum of curvature. Other special cases may occur, for instance when the second derivative is also zero, or when the curvature is constant.
    a. Vertex
    b. Coordinate-induced basis
    c. Holomorphic vector bundle
    d. Non-Euclidean crystallographic group

Chapter 12. AREAS AND VOLUMES OF SOLIDS

11. A timeline of _____ and geometry

- ca. 2000 BC -- Scotland, Carved Stone Balls exhibit a variety of symmetries including all of the symmetries of Platonic solids.
- 1800 BC -- Moscow Mathematical Papyrus, findings volume of a frustum
- 1650 BC -- Rhind Mathematical Papyrus, copy of a lost scroll from around 1850 BC, the scribe Ahmes presents one of the first known approximate values of π at 3.16, the first attempt at squaring the circle, earliest known use of a sort of cotangent, and knowledge of solving first order linear equations
- 1300 BC -- Berlin papyrus (19th dynasty) contains a quadratic equation and its solution.

- 800 BC -- Baudhayana, author of the Baudhayana Sulba Sutra, a Vedic Sanskrit geometric text, contains quadratic equations, and calculates the square root of 2 correct to five decimal places
- ca. 600 BC -- the other Vedic 'Sulba Sutras' use Pythagorean triples, contain of a number of geometrical proofs, and approximate π at 3.16
- 5th century BC -- Hippocrates of Chios utilizes lunes in an attempt to square the circle
- 5th century BC -- Apastamba, author of the Apastamba Sulba Sutra, another Vedic Sanskrit geometric text, makes an attempt at squaring the circle and also calculates the square root of 2 correct to five decimal places
- 530 BC -- Pythagoras studies propositional geometry and vibrating lyre strings; his group also discover the irrationality of the square root of two,
- 370 BC -- Eudoxus states the method of exhaustion for area determination
- 300 BC -- Euclid in his Elements studies geometry as an axiomatic system, proves the infinitude of prime numbers and presents the Euclidean algorithm; he states the law of reflection in Catoptrics, and he proves the fundamental theorem of arithmetic
- 260 BC -- Archimedes proved that the value of π lies between 3 + 1/7 and 3 + 10/71 (approx. 3.1408), that the area of a circle was equal to π multiplied by the square of the radius of the circle and that the area enclosed by a parabola and a straight line is 4/3 multiplied by the area of a triangle with equal base and height. He also gave a very accurate estimate of the value of the square root of 3.
- 225 BC -- Apollonius of Perga writes On Conic Sections and names the ellipse, parabola, and hyperbola,
- 150 BC -- Jain mathematicians in India write the 'Sthananga Sutra', which contains work on the theory of numbers, arithmetical operations, geometry, operations with fractions, simple equations, cubic equations, quartic equations, and permutations and combinations
- 140 BC -- Hipparchus develops the bases of trigonometry.

- 1st century -- Heron of Alexandria, the earliest fleeting reference to square roots of negative numbers.
- 250 -- Diophantus uses symbols for unknown numbers in terms of syncopated _____, and writes Arithmetica, one of the earliest treatises on _____
- ca. 340 -- Pappus of Alexandria states his hexagon theorem and his centroid theorem
- 500 -- Aryabhata writes the 'Aryabhata-Siddhanta', which first introduces the trigonometric functions and methods of calculating their approximate numerical values. It defines the concepts of sine and cosine, and also contains the earliest tables of sine and cosine values
- 600s -- Bhaskara I gives a rational approximation of the sine function
- 600s -- Brahmagupta invents the method of solving indeterminate equations of the second degree and is the first to use _____ to solve astronomical problems. He also develops methods for calculations of the motions and places of various planets, their rising and setting, conjunctions, and the calculation of eclipses of the sun and the moon
- 628 -- Brahmagupta writes the Brahma-sphuta-siddhanta, where zero is clearly explained, and where the modern place-value Indian numeral system is fully developed. It also gives rules for manipulating both negative and positive numbers, methods for computing square roots, methods of solving linear and quadratic equations, and rules for summing series, Brahmagupta's identity, and the Brahmagupta theorem
- 700s -- Virasena gives explicit rules for the Fibonacci sequence, gives the derivation of the volume of a frustum using an infinite procedure, and also deals with the logarithm to base 2 and knows its laws
- 700s -- Shridhara gives the rule for finding the volume of a sphere and also the formula for solving quadratic equations
- 820 -- Al-Khwarizmi -- Persian mathematician, father of _____, writes the Al-Jabr, later transliterated as _____, which introduces systematic algebraic techniques for solving linear and quadratic equations. Translations of his book on arithmetic will introduce the Hindu-Arabic decimal number system to the Western world in the 12th century.

The term algorithm is also named after him.
- 820 -- Al-Mahani conceived the idea of reducing geometrical problems such as doubling the cube to problems in _____.
- 895 -- Thabit ibn Qurra: the only surviving fragment of his original work contains a chapter on the solution and properties of cubic equations. He also generalized the Pythagorean theorem, and discovered the theorem by which pairs of amicable numbers can be found, .
- ca. 900 -- Abu Kamil of Egypt had begun to understand what we would write in symbols as $x^n \cdot x^m = x^{m+n}$
- 953 -- Al-Karaji is the 'first person to completely free _____ from geometrical operations and to replace them with the arithmetical type of operations which are at the core of _____ today. He was first to define the monomials x, x^2, x^3, … and 1 / x, 1 / x^2, 1 / x^3, … and to give rules for products of any two of these. He started a school of _____ which flourished for several hundreds of years'. He also discovered the binomial theorem for integer exponents, which 'was a major factor in the development of numerical analysis based on the decimal system.'
- 975 -- Al-Batani -- Extended the Indian concepts of sine and cosine to other trigonometrical ratios, like tangent, secant and their inverse functions. Derived the formula: $\sin \alpha = \tan \alpha / \sqrt{1 + \tan^2 \alpha}$ and $\cos \alpha = 1 / \sqrt{1 + \tan^2 \alpha}$.

- ca. 1000 -- Abū Sahl al-Qūhī (Kuhi) solves equations higher than the second degree.
- ca. 1000 -- Law of sines is discovered by Muslim mathematicians, but it is uncertain who discovers it first between Abu-Mahmud al-Khujandi, Abu Nasr Mansur, and Abu al-Wafa.
- 1070 -- Omar Khayyám begins to write Treatise on Demonstration of Problems of _____ and classifies cubic equations.
- ca. 1100 -- Omar Khayyám 'gave a complete classification of cubic equations with geometric solutions found by means of intersecting conic sections.' He became the first to find general geometric solutions of cubic equations and laid the foundations for the development of analytic geometry and non-Euclidean geometry. He also extracted roots using the decimal system .
- 1100s -- Bhaskara Acharya writes the 'Bijaganita' , which is the first text that recognizes that a positive number has two square roots
- 1130 -- Al-Samawal gave a definition of _____: '[it is concerned] with operating on unknowns using all the arithmetical tools, in the same way as the arithmetician operates on the known.'
- 1135 -- Sharafeddin Tusi followed al-Khayyam's application of _____ to geometry, and wrote a treatise on cubic equations which 'represents an essential contribution to another _____ which aimed to study curves by means of equations, thus inaugurating the beginning of algebraic geometry.'
- ca. 1250 -- Nasir Al-Din Al-Tusi attempts to develop a form of non-Euclidean geometry.
- 1400s -- Nilakantha Somayaji, a Kerala school mathematician, writes the 'Aryabhatiya Bhasya', which contains work on infinite-series expansions, problems of _____, and spherical geometry

- 1520 -- Scipione dal Ferro develops a method for solving 'depressed' cubic equations (cubic equations without an x^2 term), but does not publish.
- 1535 -- Niccolo Tartaglia independently develops a method for solving depressed cubic equations but also does not publish.
- 1539 -- Gerolamo Cardano learns Tartaglia's method for solving depressed cubics and discovers a method for depressing cubics, thereby creating a method for solving all cubics.
- 1540 -- Lodovico Ferrari solves the quartic equation.

- 1600s - Putumana Somayaji writes the 'Paddhati', which presents a detailed discussion of various trigonometric series
- 1619 - René Descartes discovers analytic geometry (Pierre de Fermat claimed that he also discovered it independently),
- 1619 - Johannes Kepler discovers two of the Kepler-Poinsot polyhedra.
- 1637 - Pierre de Fermat claims to have proven Fermat's Last Theorem in his copy of Diophantus' Arithmetica,
- 1637 - First use of the term imaginary number by René Descartes; it was meant to be derogatory.

- 1722 - Abraham de Moivre states de Moivre's formula connecting trigonometric functions and complex numbers,
- 1733 - Giovanni Gerolamo Saccheri studies what geometry would be like if Euclid's fifth postulate were false,
- 1796 - Carl Friedrich Gauss proves that the regular 17-gon can be constructed using only a compass and straightedge
- 1797 - Caspar Wessel associates vectors with complex numbers and studies complex number operations in geometrical terms,
- 1799 - Carl Friedrich Gauss proves the fundamental theorem of _____,

- 1799 - Paolo Ruffini partially proves the Abel-Ruffini theorem that quintic or higher equations cannot be solved by a general formula,

- 1806 - Louis Poinsot discovers the two remaining Kepler-Poinsot polyhedra.
- 1806 - Jean-Robert Argand publishes proof of the Fundamental theorem of _____ and the Argand diagram,
- 1824 - Niels Henrik Abel partially proves the Abel-Ruffini theorem that the general quintic or higher equations cannot be solved by a general formula involving only arithmetical operations and roots,
- 1829 - Bolyai, Gauss, and Lobachevsky invent hyperbolic non-Euclidean geometry,
- 1832 - Évariste Galois presents a general condition for the solvability of algebraic equations, thereby essentially founding group theory and Galois theory,
- 1837 - Pierre Wantsel proves that doubling the cube and trisecting the angle are impossible with only a compass and straightedge, as well as the full completion of the problem of constructability of regular polygons
- 1843 - William Hamilton discovers the calculus of quaternions and deduces that they are non-commutative,
- 1847 - George Boole formalizes symbolic logic in The Mathematical Analysis of Logic, defining what now is called Boolean _____,
- 1854 - Bernhard Riemann introduces Riemannian geometry,
- 1854 - Arthur Cayley shows that quaternions can be used to represent rotations in four-dimensional space,
- 1858 - August Ferdinand Möbius invents the Möbius strip,
- 1870 - Felix Klein constructs an analytic geometry for Lobachevski's geometry thereby establishing its self-consistency and the logical independence of Euclid's fifth postulate,
- 1873 - Charles Hermite proves that e is transcendental,
- 1878 - Charles Hermite solves the general quintic equation by means of elliptic and modular functions
- 1882 - Ferdinand von Lindemann proves that π is transcendental and that therefore the circle cannot be squared with a compass and straightedge,
- 1882 - Felix Klein invents the Klein bottle,
- 1899 - David Hilbert presents a set of self-consistent geometric axioms in Foundations of Geometry,

- 1901 - Élie Cartan develops the exterior derivative,
- 1905 - Einstein's theory of special relativity.
- 1912 - Luitzen Egbertus Jan Brouwer presents the Brouwer fixed-point theorem,
- 1916 - Einstein's theory of general relativity.
- 1930 - Casimir Kuratowski shows that the three-cottage problem has no solution,
- 1931 - Georges de Rham develops theorems in cohomology and characteristic classes,
- 1933 - Karol Borsuk and Stanislaw Ulam present the Borsuk-Ulam antipodal-point theorem,
- 1955 - H. S. M. Coxeter et al. publish the complete list of uniform polyhedron,
- 1981 - Mikhail Gromov develops the theory of hyperbolic groups, revolutionizing both infinite group theory and global differential geometry,
- 1983 - the classification of finite simple groups, a collaborative work involving some hundred mathematicians and spanning thirty years, is completed,
- 1991 - Alain Connes and John W. Lott develop non-commutative geometry,
- 1998 - Thomas Callister Hales (almost certainly) proves the Kepler conjecture,

- 2003 - Grigori Perelman proves the Poincaré conjecture,
- 2007 - a team of researches throughout North America and Europe used networks of computers to map E8 (mathematics.)

Chapter 12. AREAS AND VOLUMES OF SOLIDS

a. AA postulate
c. ADHM construction

b. ADE classification
d. Algebra

12. In geometry and trigonometry, an _____ is the figure formed by two rays sharing a common endpoint, called the vertex of the _____ . The magnitude of the _____ is the 'amount of rotation' that separates the two rays, and can be measured by considering the length of circular arc swept out when one ray is rotated about the vertex to coincide with the other Where there is no possibility of confusion, the term '_____' is used interchangeably for both the geometric configuration itself and for its angular magnitude (which is simply a numerical quantity.)

a. AA postulate
c. ADE classification

b. ADHM construction
d. Angle

13. In mathematics, a _____ is a flat surface. _____s can arise as subspaces of some higher dimensional space, as with the walls of a room, or they may enjoy an independent existence in their own right, as in the setting of Euclidean geometry

a. Simple polytope
c. Parallelogram law

b. Pendent
d. Plane

14. _____ is the boundless, three-dimensional extent in which objects and events occur and have relative position and direction. Physical _____ is often conceived in three linear dimensions, although modern physicists usually consider it, with time, to be part of the boundless four-dimensional continuum known as spacetime. In mathematics _____s with different numbers of dimensions and with different underlying structures can be examined.

a. 1-center problem
c. Space

b. 11-cell
d. -module

15. A _____ is a simple shape of Euclidean geometry consisting of those points in a plane which are the same distance from a given point called the centre. The common distance of the points of a _____ from its center is called its radius.

_____s are simple closed curves which divide the plane into two regions, an interior and an exterior.

a. 1-center problem
c. Circle

b. 11-cell
d. -module

16. An _____ has the top and bottom surfaces displaced from one another.

There are other more unusual types of cylinders. These are the imaginary elliptic cylinders:

$$\left(\frac{x}{a}\right)^2 + \left(\frac{y}{b}\right)^2 = -1$$

the hyperbolic cylinder:

$$\left(\frac{x}{a}\right)^2 - \left(\frac{y}{b}\right)^2 = 1$$

and the parabolic cylinder:

$$x^2 + 2ay = 0.$$

  a. Oblique Cylinder
  c. ADHM construction
  b. AA postulate
  d. ADE classification

17. A _____ is a movement of an object in a circular motion. A two-dimensional object rotates around a center (or point) of _____. A three-dimensional object rotates around a line called an axis.
  a. Similarity
  c. Curve of constant width
  b. Rotation
  d. Square lattice

18. In geometry, an _____ planar shape or solid is one that is enclosed by and 'fits snugly' inside another geometric shape or solid. Specifically, at all points where figures meet, their edges must lie tangent. There must be no object similar to the _____ object but larger and also enclosed by the outer figure.
  a. Octomino
  c. Order-4 dodecahedral honeycomb
  b. Isometry group
  d. Inscribed

19. In every _____ there is a cuboid with all vertices tangent to the surface of said _____. It immediately becomes apparent that the cuboid inscribed in the _____ must be a cube with all vertices tangent to the surface of the _____.

Formula 1, shown below, finds the length of one side of the inscribed cube, and Formula 2 finds the volume of the inscribed cube.

  a. Circumference
  c. Cone
  b. Point group in two dimensions
  d. Sphere

20. A _____ is a path that surrounds an area. The word comes from the Greek peri and meter (measure.) The term may be used either for the path or its length.
  a. Transversal line
  c. Perimeter
  b. Complementary angles
  d. Multilateration

21. In mathematics, a _____ is a generalization of the notion of a 'straight line' to 'curved spaces'. In the presence of a metric, _____s are defined to be (locally) the shortest path between points on the space. In the presence of an affine connection, _____s are defined to be curves whose tangent vectors remain parallel if they are transported along it.
  a. Minkowski space
  c. Geodesic
  b. Gauge theory
  d. Volume

22. The mathematical object 'chord' of the 'geodesic sphere' corresponds to the structural 'strut' of the physical '_____'. The general definition of a chord is a (straight) line segment joining two points on a curve. For simple _____s we recognize the associated curve to be the surface of a sphere.

Chapter 12. AREAS AND VOLUMES OF SOLIDS

a. 1-center problem
c. 11-cell
b. -module
d. Geodesic dome

23. In mathematics, a _____ is a closed geometrical surface which can be obtained by sectioning off a portion of a sphere with an intersecting plane. It consists of two parts: (1) a flat disk, which is joined to (2) a convex surface whose curvature is uniform and which has a circular boundary: this boundary joins with the rim of the disk. The disk can be referred to as the _____'s 'base'.
a. Tomahawk
c. Lens
b. Trilon
d. Dome

24. In geometry, an _____ is any polyhedron having 20 faces, but usually a regular _____ is implied, which has equilateral triangles as faces.

The regular _____ is one of the five Platonic solids. It is a convex regular polyhedron composed of twenty triangular faces, with five meeting at each of the twelve vertices.

a. ADE classification
c. ADHM construction
b. AA postulate
d. Icosahedron

25. An _____ is a polyhedron with eight faces. A regular _____ is a Platonic solid composed of eight equilateral triangles, four of which meet at each vertex.
a. AA postulate
c. ADHM construction
b. ADE classification
d. Octahedron

26. A _____ is an expression which compares quantities relative to each other. The most common examples involve two quantities, but in theory any number of quantities can be compared. In mathematical terms, they are represented by separating each quantity with a colon, for example the _____ 2:3, which is read as the _____ 'two to three'.
a. Slope of a line
c. -module
b. Slope
d. Ratio

27. One of the meanings of the terms _____ and _____ transformation (also called dilation) of a Euclidean space is a function f from the space into itself that multiplies all distances by the same positive scalar r, so that for any two points x and y we have

$$d(f(x), f(y)) = rd(x,y),$$

where 'd(x,y)' is the Euclidean distance from x to y. Two sets are called similar if one is the image of the other under such a _____.

A special case is a homothetic transformation or central _____: it neither involves rotation nor taking the mirror image.

a. Square lattice
c. Similarity
b. Flat
d. Similar

Chapter 12. AREAS AND VOLUMES OF SOLIDS

28. Two geometrical objects are called _____ if they both have the same shape. Equivalently and more precisely, one is congruent to the result of a uniform scaling (enlarging or shrinking) of the other. Corresponding sides of _____ polygons are in proportion, and corresponding angles of _____ polygons have the same measure.
   a. Simple polytope
   b. Plane
   c. Steiner-Lehmus theorem
   d. Similar

29. An _____ describes the structure and behaviour of applications used in a business, focused on how they interact with each other and with users. It is focused on the data consumed and produced by applications rather than their internal structure. In application portfolio management, the applications are usually mapped to business functions and to application platform technologies.
   a. ADHM construction
   b. ADE classification
   c. AA postulate
   d. Applications architecture

30. In Euclidean geometry, a _____ is a quadrilateral with four right angles. Equivalently, it is an equiangular quadrilateral, but it is not necessarily equilateral.

A _____ with vertices ABCD would be denoted as ABCD.

- All angles are 90 degrees.
- Opposite sides are equal in length.
- Opposite sides are parallel.
- Diagonals are equal in length and bisect each other.

The formula for the perimeter of a _____.

If a _____ has length l and width w

- it has area A = lw
- perimeter P = 2l + 2w = 2(l + w)
- and each diagonal has length $\sqrt{l^2 + w^2}$.

When the length is equal to the width, the _____ is a square.

   a. -module
   b. 1-center problem
   c. 11-cell
   d. Rectangle

31. A _____ is one of the basic shapes of geometry: a polygon with three corners or vertices and three sides or edges which are line segments. A _____ with vertices A, B, and C is denoted ABC.

In Euclidean geometry any three non-collinear points determine a unique _____ and a unique plane (i.e. a two-dimensional Euclidean space.)

   a. 1-center problem
   b. Triangle
   c. 11-cell
   d. -module

Chapter 13. COORDINATE GEOMETRY

1. A timeline of _____ and geometry

    - ca. 2000 BC -- Scotland, Carved Stone Balls exhibit a variety of symmetries including all of the symmetries of Platonic solids.
    - 1800 BC -- Moscow Mathematical Papyrus, findings volume of a frustum
    - 1650 BC -- Rhind Mathematical Papyrus, copy of a lost scroll from around 1850 BC, the scribe Ahmes presents one of the first known approximate values of π at 3.16, the first attempt at squaring the circle, earliest known use of a sort of cotangent, and knowledge of solving first order linear equations
    - 1300 BC -- Berlin papyrus (19th dynasty) contains a quadratic equation and its solution.

    - 800 BC -- Baudhayana, author of the Baudhayana Sulba Sutra, a Vedic Sanskrit geometric text, contains quadratic equations, and calculates the square root of 2 correct to five decimal places
    - ca. 600 BC -- the other Vedic 'Sulba Sutras' use Pythagorean triples, contain of a number of geometrical proofs, and approximate π at 3.16
    - 5th century BC -- Hippocrates of Chios utilizes lunes in an attempt to square the circle
    - 5th century BC -- Apastamba, author of the Apastamba Sulba Sutra, another Vedic Sanskrit geometric text, makes an attempt at squaring the circle and also calculates the square root of 2 correct to five decimal places
    - 530 BC -- Pythagoras studies propositional geometry and vibrating lyre strings; his group also discover the irrationality of the square root of two,
    - 370 BC -- Eudoxus states the method of exhaustion for area determination
    - 300 BC -- Euclid in his Elements studies geometry as an axiomatic system, proves the infinitude of prime numbers and presents the Euclidean algorithm; he states the law of reflection in Catoptrics, and he proves the fundamental theorem of arithmetic
    - 260 BC -- Archimedes proved that the value of π lies between 3 + 1/7 and 3 + 10/71 (approx. 3.1408), that the area of a circle was equal to π multiplied by the square of the radius of the circle and that the area enclosed by a parabola and a straight line is 4/3 multiplied by the area of a triangle with equal base and height. He also gave a very accurate estimate of the value of the square root of 3.
    - 225 BC -- Apollonius of Perga writes On Conic Sections and names the ellipse, parabola, and hyperbola,
    - 150 BC -- Jain mathematicians in India write the 'Sthananga Sutra', which contains work on the theory of numbers, arithmetical operations, geometry, operations with fractions, simple equations, cubic equations, quartic equations, and permutations and combinations
    - 140 BC -- Hipparchus develops the bases of trigonometry.

    - 1st century -- Heron of Alexandria, the earliest fleeting reference to square roots of negative numbers.
    - 250 -- Diophantus uses symbols for unknown numbers in terms of syncopated _____, and writes Arithmetica, one of the earliest treatises on _____
    - ca. 340 -- Pappus of Alexandria states his hexagon theorem and his centroid theorem
    - 500 -- Aryabhata writes the 'Aryabhata-Siddhanta', which first introduces the trigonometric functions and methods of calculating their approximate numerical values. It defines the concepts of sine and cosine, and also contains the earliest tables of sine and cosine values
    - 600s -- Bhaskara I gives a rational approximation of the sine function
    - 600s -- Brahmagupta invents the method of solving indeterminate equations of the second degree and is the first to use _____ to solve astronomical problems. He also develops methods for calculations of the motions and places of various planets, their rising and setting, conjunctions, and the calculation of eclipses of the sun and the moon
    - 628 -- Brahmagupta writes the Brahma-sphuta-siddhanta, where zero is clearly explained, and where the modern place-value Indian numeral system is fully developed. It also gives rules for manipulating both negative and positive numbers, methods for computing square roots, methods of solving linear and quadratic equations, and rules for summing series, Brahmagupta's identity, and the Brahmagupta theorem
    - 700s -- Virasena gives explicit rules for the Fibonacci sequence, gives the derivation of the volume of a frustum using an infinite procedure, and also deals with the logarithm to base 2 and knows its laws
    - 700s -- Shridhara gives the rule for finding the volume of a sphere and also the formula for solving quadratic equations
    - 820 -- Al-Khwarizmi -- Persian mathematician, father of _____, writes the Al-Jabr, later transliterated as _____, which introduces systematic algebraic techniques for solving linear and quadratic equations. Translations of his book on arithmetic will introduce the Hindu-Arabic decimal number system to the Western world in the 12th century.

The term algorithm is also named after him.
- 820 -- Al-Mahani conceived the idea of reducing geometrical problems such as doubling the cube to problems in _____.
- 895 -- Thabit ibn Qurra: the only surviving fragment of his original work contains a chapter on the solution and properties of cubic equations. He also generalized the Pythagorean theorem, and discovered the theorem by which pairs of amicable numbers can be found, .
- ca. 900 -- Abu Kamil of Egypt had begun to understand what we would write in symbols as $x^n \cdot x^m = x^{m+n}$
- 953 -- Al-Karaji is the 'first person to completely free _____ from geometrical operations and to replace them with the arithmetical type of operations which are at the core of _____ today. He was first to define the monomials x, x^2, x^3, â€¦ and 1 / x, 1 / x^2, 1 / x^3, â€¦ and to give rules for products of any two of these. He started a school of _____ which flourished for several hundreds of years'. He also discovered the binomial theorem for integer exponents, which 'was a major factor in the development of numerical analysis based on the decimal system.'
- 975 -- Al-Batani -- Extended the Indian concepts of sine and cosine to other trigonometrical ratios, like tangent, secant and their inverse functions. Derived the formula: $\sin\alpha = \tan\alpha / \sqrt{1 + \tan^2\alpha}$ and $\cos\alpha = 1 / \sqrt{1 + \tan^2\alpha}$.

- ca. 1000 -- AbÅ« Sahl al-QÅ«hÄ« (Kuhi) solves equations higher than the second degree.
- ca. 1000 -- Law of sines is discovered by Muslim mathematicians, but it is uncertain who discovers it first between Abu-Mahmud al-Khujandi, Abu Nasr Mansur, and Abu al-Wafa.
- 1070 -- Omar Khayyám begins to write Treatise on Demonstration of Problems of _____ and classifies cubic equations.
- ca. 1100 -- Omar Khayyám 'gave a complete classification of cubic equations with geometric solutions found by means of intersecting conic sections.' He became the first to find general geometric solutions of cubic equations and laid the foundations for the development of analytic geometry and non-Euclidean geometry. He also extracted roots using the decimal system .
- 1100s -- Bhaskara Acharya writes the 'Bijaganita' , which is the first text that recognizes that a positive number has two square roots
- 1130 -- Al-Samawal gave a definition of _____: '[it is concerned] with operating on unknowns using all the arithmetical tools, in the same way as the arithmetician operates on the known.'
- 1135 -- Sharafeddin Tusi followed al-Khayyam's application of _____ to geometry, and wrote a treatise on cubic equations which 'represents an essential contribution to another _____ which aimed to study curves by means of equations, thus inaugurating the beginning of algebraic geometry.'
- ca. 1250 -- Nasir Al-Din Al-Tusi attempts to develop a form of non-Euclidean geometry.
- 1400s -- Nilakantha Somayaji, a Kerala school mathematician, writes the 'Aryabhatiya Bhasya', which contains work on infinite-series expansions, problems of _____, and spherical geometry

- 1520 -- Scipione dal Ferro develops a method for solving 'depressed' cubic equations (cubic equations without an x^2 term), but does not publish.
- 1535 -- Niccolo Tartaglia independently develops a method for solving depressed cubic equations but also does not publish.
- 1539 -- Gerolamo Cardano learns Tartaglia's method for solving depressed cubics and discovers a method for depressing cubics, thereby creating a method for solving all cubics.
- 1540 -- Lodovico Ferrari solves the quartic equation.

- 1600s - Putumana Somayaji writes the 'Paddhati', which presents a detailed discussion of various trigonometric series
- 1619 - René Descartes discovers analytic geometry (Pierre de Fermat claimed that he also discovered it independently),
- 1619 - Johannes Kepler discovers two of the Kepler-Poinsot polyhedra.
- 1637 - Pierre de Fermat claims to have proven Fermat's Last Theorem in his copy of Diophantus' Arithmetica,
- 1637 - First use of the term imaginary number by René Descartes; it was meant to be derogatory.

- 1722 - Abraham de Moivre states de Moivre's formula connecting trigonometric functions and complex numbers,
- 1733 - Giovanni Gerolamo Saccheri studies what geometry would be like if Euclid's fifth postulate were false,
- 1796 - Carl Friedrich Gauss proves that the regular 17-gon can be constructed using only a compass and straightedge
- 1797 - Caspar Wessel associates vectors with complex numbers and studies complex number operations in geometrical terms,
- 1799 - Carl Friedrich Gauss proves the fundamental theorem of _____,

- 1799 - Paolo Ruffini partially proves the Abel-Ruffini theorem that quintic or higher equations cannot be solved by a general formula,

- 1806 - Louis Poinsot discovers the two remaining Kepler-Poinsot polyhedra.
- 1806 - Jean-Robert Argand publishes proof of the Fundamental theorem of _____ and the Argand diagram,
- 1824 - Niels Henrik Abel partially proves the Abel-Ruffini theorem that the general quintic or higher equations cannot be solved by a general formula involving only arithmetical operations and roots,
- 1829 - Bolyai, Gauss, and Lobachevsky invent hyperbolic non-Euclidean geometry,
- 1832 - Évariste Galois presents a general condition for the solvability of algebraic equations, thereby essentially founding group theory and Galois theory,
- 1837 - Pierre Wantsel proves that doubling the cube and trisecting the angle are impossible with only a compass and straightedge, as well as the full completion of the problem of constructability of regular polygons
- 1843 - William Hamilton discovers the calculus of quaternions and deduces that they are non-commutative,
- 1847 - George Boole formalizes symbolic logic in The Mathematical Analysis of Logic, defining what now is called Boolean _____,
- 1854 - Bernhard Riemann introduces Riemannian geometry,
- 1854 - Arthur Cayley shows that quaternions can be used to represent rotations in four-dimensional space,
- 1858 - August Ferdinand Möbius invents the Möbius strip,
- 1870 - Felix Klein constructs an analytic geometry for Lobachevski's geometry thereby establishing its self-consistency and the logical independence of Euclid's fifth postulate,
- 1873 - Charles Hermite proves that e is transcendental,
- 1878 - Charles Hermite solves the general quintic equation by means of elliptic and modular functions
- 1882 - Ferdinand von Lindemann proves that π is transcendental and that therefore the circle cannot be squared with a compass and straightedge,
- 1882 - Felix Klein invents the Klein bottle,
- 1899 - David Hilbert presents a set of self-consistent geometric axioms in Foundations of Geometry,

- 1901 - Élie Cartan develops the exterior derivative,
- 1905 - Einstein's theory of special relativity.
- 1912 - Luitzen Egbertus Jan Brouwer presents the Brouwer fixed-point theorem,
- 1916 - Einstein's theory of general relativity.
- 1930 - Casimir Kuratowski shows that the three-cottage problem has no solution,
- 1931 - Georges de Rham develops theorems in cohomology and characteristic classes,
- 1933 - Karol Borsuk and Stanislaw Ulam present the Borsuk-Ulam antipodal-point theorem,
- 1955 - H. S. M. Coxeter et al. publish the complete list of uniform polyhedron,
- 1981 - Mikhail Gromov develops the theory of hyperbolic groups, revolutionizing both infinite group theory and global differential geometry,
- 1983 - the classification of finite simple groups, a collaborative work involving some hundred mathematicians and spanning thirty years, is completed,
- 1991 - Alain Connes and John W. Lott develop non-commutative geometry,
- 1998 - Thomas Callister Hales (almost certainly) proves the Kepler conjecture,

- 2003 - Grigori Perelman proves the Poincaré conjecture,
- 2007 - a team of researches throughout North America and Europe used networks of computers to map E8 (mathematics.)

Chapter 13. COORDINATE GEOMETRY

a. ADHM construction
b. AA postulate
c. ADE classification
d. Algebra

2. A _____ is a number that determines the location of a point along some line or curve. A list of two, three, or more _____s can be used to determine the location of a point on a surface, volume, or higher-dimensional domain.

For example, the longitude is a _____ which determines the position of a point along the Earth's equator, and latitude is another _____ that defines a poisition along a meridian.

a. 1-center problem
b. 11-cell
c. -module
d. Coordinate

3. In mathematics, an _____ is a collection of objects having two coordinates (or entries or projections), such that one can always uniquely determine the object, which is the first coordinate (or first entry or left projection) of the pair as well as the second coordinate (or second entry or right projection.) If the first coordinate is a and the second is b, the usual notation for an _____ is (a, b.) The pair is 'ordered' in that (a, b) differs from (b, a) unless a = b.

a. ADE classification
b. AA postulate
c. ADHM construction
d. Ordered pair

4. In mathematics, the _____ of a Euclidean space is a special point, usually denoted by the letter O, used as a fixed point of reference for the geometry of the surrounding space. In a Cartesian coordinate system, the _____ is the point where the axes of the system intersect. In Euclidean geometry, the _____ may be chosen freely as any convenient point of reference.

a. Adams-hemisphere-in-a-square
b. Apollonius' theorem
c. Origin
d. Apex

5. In mathematics, a _____ is a flat surface. _____s can arise as subspaces of some higher dimensional space, as with the walls of a room, or they may enjoy an independent existence in their own right, as in the setting of Euclidean geometry

a. Pendent
b. Plane
c. Simple polytope
d. Parallelogram law

6. In geometry, topology and related branches of mathematics a spatial _____ describes a specific object within a given space that consists of neither volume, area, length, nor any other higher dimensional analogue. Thus, a _____ is a 0-dimensional object. Because of their nature as one of the simplest geometric concepts, they are often used in one form or another as the fundamental constituents of geometry, physics, vector graphics, and many other fields.

a. 11-cell
b. 1-center problem
c. Point
d. -module

7. In mathematics, the _____ of a real number is its numerical value without regard to its sign. So, for example, 3 is the _____ of both 3 and −3.

The _____ of a number a is denoted by $|a|$.

a. AA postulate
b. Absolute value
c. ADHM construction
d. ADE classification

8. In mathematics, a (B, N) _____ is a structure on groups of Lie type that allows one to give uniform proofs of many results, instead of giving a large number of case-by-case proofs. Roughly speaking, it shows that all such groups are similar to the general linear group over a field. They were invented by the mathematician Jacques Tits, and are also sometimes known as Tits systems.
   a. Dihedral group
   b. Free group
   c. Hanna Neumann conjecture
   d. Pair

9. A _____ is a simple shape of Euclidean geometry consisting of those points in a plane which are the same distance from a given point called the centre. The common distance of the points of a _____ from its center is called its radius.

_____s are simple closed curves which divide the plane into two regions, an interior and an exterior.

   a. 11-cell
   b. -module
   c. 1-center problem
   d. Circle

10. _____ is used to describe the steepness, incline, gradient, or grade of a straight line. A higher _____ value indicates a steeper incline. The _____ is defined as the ratio of the 'rise' divided by the 'run' between two points on a line, or in other words, the ratio of the altitude change to the horizontal distance between any two points on the line.
    a. -module
    b. Sequence
    c. Slope of a line
    d. Slope

11. The _____ is defined as the rise over the run, .
    a. -module
    b. Sequence
    c. Slope
    d. Slope of a line

12. In chemistry, the _____ molecular geometry describes the arrangement of three or more atoms placed at an expected bond angle of 180Å°. _____ organic molecules, e.g. acetylene, are often described by invoking sp orbital hybridization for the carbon centers. Many _____ molecules exist, prominent examples include CO_2, HCN, and xenon difluoride.
    a. -module
    b. 11-cell
    c. 1-center problem
    d. Linear

13. where a is any scalar. A function which satisfies these properties is called a linear function, or more generally a linear map. This property makes _____s particularly easy to solve and reason about.
    a. 1-center problem
    b. 11-cell
    c. Linear equation
    d. -module

14. _____ is the study of mathematical structures that are fundamentally discrete rather than continuous. Real numbers and rational numbers have the property that between any two numbers a third can be found, and consequently these numbers vary 'smoothly'. The objects generally studied in _____ - such as integers, graphs, and statements in logic - do not vary smoothly in this way, but have distinct, separated values.

a. Discrete mathematics
b. -module
c. 1-center problem
d. 11-cell

15. In geometry, the _____ line (or simply the _____) to a curve at a given point is the straight line that 'just touches' the curve at that point (in the sense explained more precisely below.) As it passes through the point of tangency, the _____ line is 'going in the same direction' as the curve, and in this sense it is the best straight-line approximation to the curve at that point. The same definition applies to space curves and curves in n-dimensional Euclidean space.
a. Cartan connection
b. Tangent
c. Metric signature
d. Measuring function

16. A _____ is an expression which compares quantities relative to each other. The most common examples involve two quantities, but in theory any number of quantities can be compared. In mathematical terms, they are represented by separating each quantity with a colon, for example the _____ 2:3, which is read as the _____ 'two to three'.
a. Slope of a line
b. Ratio
c. Slope
d. -module

17. In each statement above, a is not equal to b. These relations are known as strict _____. The notation a < b may also be read as 'a is strictly less than b'.
a. AA postulate
b. ADE classification
c. ADHM construction
d. Inequalities

18. A _____ is an instrument used in geometry, technical drawing and engineering/building to measure distances and/or to rule straight lines. Strictly speaking, the _____ is essentially a straightedge used to rule lines and the calibrated instrument used for determining measurement is called a 'measure'. However, common usage is that a _____ is a calibrated straightedge that can be used for making measurements.
a. 1-center problem
b. -module
c. 11-cell
d. Ruler

19. A _____ of a curve is the envelope of a family of congruent circles centered on the curve. It generalises the concept of _____ lines.

It is sometimes called the offset curve but the term 'offset' often refers also to translation.
a. Parallel
b. Cissoid
c. Trisectrix of Maclaurin
d. Cassini oval

20. In mathematics, a _____ is a convincing demonstration (within the accepted standards of the field) that some mathematical statement is necessarily true. _____s are obtained from deductive reasoning, rather than from inductive or empirical arguments. That is, a _____ must demonstrate that a statement is true in all cases, without a single exception.
a. Proof
b. Logical axioms
c. Theorem
d. Contrapositive

21. In logic, _____ is a form of proof that establishes the truth or validity of a proposition by demonstrating the truth or validity of the converse of its negated parts.

Chapter 13. COORDINATE GEOMETRY

In other words, to prove by contraposition that $P \Rightarrow Q$, prove that $\neg Q \Rightarrow \neg P$.

a. 11-cell
b. -module
c. Proof by contrapositive
d. 1-center problem

22. In vernacular terms, this states 'If P then Q', or, 'If Socrates is a man then Socrates is human.' In a conditional such as this, P is called the antecedent and Q the consequent. One statement is the _____ of the other just when its antecedent is the negated consequent of the other, and vice-versa. The _____ of the given example statement would be:

$$(\neg Q \to \neg P)$$

That is, 'If not-Q then not-P', or more clearly, 'If Q is not the case, then P is not the case.' Using our example, this is rendered 'If Socrates is not human, then Socrates is not a man.' This statement is said to be contraposed to the original, and is logically equivalent to it.

a. Logical axioms
b. Logically equivalent
c. Theorem
d. Contrapositive

23. The _____ is the middle point of a line segment. It is equidistant from both endpoints. The formula for determining the _____ of a segment in the plane, with endpoints and is

$$\left(\frac{x_1 + x_2}{2}, \frac{y_1 + y_2}{2}\right).$$

In three-dimensional Cartesian space, the _____ formula is

$$\left(\frac{x_1 + x_2}{2}, \frac{y_1 + y_2}{2}, \frac{z_1 + z_2}{2}\right).$$

_____ used in algebra 1=rectangles _____ used in algebra 2=triangles _____ used in geometry=circles

- Astrology _____ s
- Median
- Segment bisector
- Numerical Integration

a. Parallel postulate
b. Quincunx
c. Midpoint
d. Golden angle

24. In geometry, the circumscribed circle or circumcircle of a polygon is a circle which passes through all the vertices of the polygon. The center of this circle is called the _____.

A polygon which has a circumscribed circle is called a cyclic polygon.

a. Circumscribed
b. Circular sector
c. Circumcenter
d. Nine-Point Circle

25. Analytic geometry, usually called _____ and earlier referred to as Cartesian geometry or analytical geometry, is the study of geometry using the principles of algebra; the modern development of analytic geometry is thus suggestively called algebraic geometry.

Usually the Cartesian coordinate system is applied to manipulate equations for planes, straight lines, and squares, often in two and sometimes in three dimensions of measurement. Geometrical, one studies the Euclidean plane (2 dimensions) and Euclidean space (3 dimensions.)

a. Coordinate geometry
b. Fredholm module
c. Coaxial
d. Gyroid

26. The three altitudes intersect in a single point, called the _____ of the triangle. The _____ lies inside the triangle (and consequently the feet of the altitudes all fall on the triangle) if and only if the triangle is not obtuse (i.e. does not have an angle greater than a right angle.) See also orthocentric system.

a. Equilateral triangle
b. AA postulate
c. ADE classification
d. Orthocenter

27. _____ is the boundless, three-dimensional extent in which objects and events occur and have relative position and direction. Physical _____ is often conceived in three linear dimensions, although modern physicists usually consider it, with time, to be part of the boundless four-dimensional continuum known as spacetime. In mathematics _____s with different numbers of dimensions and with different underlying structures can be examined.

a. -module
b. 11-cell
c. 1-center problem
d. Space

Chapter 14. TRANSFORMATIONS

1. A timeline of _____ and geometry

   - ca. 2000 BC -- Scotland, Carved Stone Balls exhibit a variety of symmetries including all of the symmetries of Platonic solids.
   - 1800 BC -- Moscow Mathematical Papyrus, findings volume of a frustum
   - 1650 BC -- Rhind Mathematical Papyrus, copy of a lost scroll from around 1850 BC, the scribe Ahmes presents one of the first known approximate values of π at 3.16, the first attempt at squaring the circle, earliest known use of a sort of cotangent, and knowledge of solving first order linear equations
   - 1300 BC -- Berlin papyrus (19th dynasty) contains a quadratic equation and its solution.

   - 800 BC -- Baudhayana, author of the Baudhayana Sulba Sutra, a Vedic Sanskrit geometric text, contains quadratic equations, and calculates the square root of 2 correct to five decimal places
   - ca. 600 BC -- the other Vedic 'Sulba Sutras' use Pythagorean triples, contain of a number of geometrical proofs, and approximate π at 3.16
   - 5th century BC -- Hippocrates of Chios utilizes lunes in an attempt to square the circle
   - 5th century BC -- Apastamba, author of the Apastamba Sulba Sutra, another Vedic Sanskrit geometric text, makes an attempt at squaring the circle and also calculates the square root of 2 correct to five decimal places
   - 530 BC -- Pythagoras studies propositional geometry and vibrating lyre strings; his group also discover the irrationality of the square root of two,
   - 370 BC -- Eudoxus states the method of exhaustion for area determination
   - 300 BC -- Euclid in his Elements studies geometry as an axiomatic system, proves the infinitude of prime numbers and presents the Euclidean algorithm; he states the law of reflection in Catoptrics, and he proves the fundamental theorem of arithmetic
   - 260 BC -- Archimedes proved that the value of π lies between 3 + 1/7 and 3 + 10/71 (approx. 3.1408), that the area of a circle was equal to π multiplied by the square of the radius of the circle and that the area enclosed by a parabola and a straight line is 4/3 multiplied by the area of a triangle with equal base and height. He also gave a very accurate estimate of the value of the square root of 3.
   - 225 BC -- Apollonius of Perga writes On Conic Sections and names the ellipse, parabola, and hyperbola,
   - 150 BC -- Jain mathematicians in India write the 'Sthananga Sutra', which contains work on the theory of numbers, arithmetical operations, geometry, operations with fractions, simple equations, cubic equations, quartic equations, and permutations and combinations
   - 140 BC -- Hipparchus develops the bases of trigonometry.

   - 1st century -- Heron of Alexandria, the earliest fleeting reference to square roots of negative numbers.
   - 250 -- Diophantus uses symbols for unknown numbers in terms of syncopated _____, and writes Arithmetica, one of the earliest treatises on _____
   - ca. 340 -- Pappus of Alexandria states his hexagon theorem and his centroid theorem
   - 500 -- Aryabhata writes the 'Aryabhata-Siddhanta', which first introduces the trigonometric functions and methods of calculating their approximate numerical values. It defines the concepts of sine and cosine, and also contains the earliest tables of sine and cosine values
   - 600s -- Bhaskara I gives a rational approximation of the sine function
   - 600s -- Brahmagupta invents the method of solving indeterminate equations of the second degree and is the first to use _____ to solve astronomical problems. He also develops methods for calculations of the motions and places of various planets, their rising and setting, conjunctions, and the calculation of eclipses of the sun and the moon
   - 628 -- Brahmagupta writes the Brahma-sphuta-siddhanta, where zero is clearly explained, and where the modern place-value Indian numeral system is fully developed. It also gives rules for manipulating both negative and positive numbers, methods for computing square roots, methods of solving linear and quadratic equations, and rules for summing series, Brahmagupta's identity, and the Brahmagupta theorem
   - 700s -- Virasena gives explicit rules for the Fibonacci sequence, gives the derivation of the volume of a frustum using an infinite procedure, and also deals with the logarithm to base 2 and knows its laws
   - 700s -- Shridhara gives the rule for finding the volume of a sphere and also the formula for solving quadratic equations
   - 820 -- Al-Khwarizmi -- Persian mathematician, father of _____, writes the Al-Jabr, later transliterated as _____, which introduces systematic algebraic techniques for solving linear and quadratic equations. Translations of his book on arithmetic will introduce the Hindu-Arabic decimal number system to the Western world in the 12th century.

The term algorithm is also named after him.
- 820 -- Al-Mahani conceived the idea of reducing geometrical problems such as doubling the cube to problems in _____.
- 895 -- Thabit ibn Qurra: the only surviving fragment of his original work contains a chapter on the solution and properties of cubic equations. He also generalized the Pythagorean theorem, and discovered the theorem by which pairs of amicable numbers can be found, .
- ca. 900 -- Abu Kamil of Egypt had begun to understand what we would write in symbols as $x^n \cdot x^m = x^{m+n}$
- 953 -- Al-Karaji is the 'first person to completely free _____ from geometrical operations and to replace them with the arithmetical type of operations which are at the core of _____ today. He was first to define the monomials x, x^2, x^3, â€¦ and 1 / x, 1 / x^2, 1 / x^3, â€¦ and to give rules for products of any two of these. He started a school of _____ which flourished for several hundreds of years'. He also discovered the binomial theorem for integer exponents, which 'was a major factor in the development of numerical analysis based on the decimal system.'
- 975 -- Al-Batani -- Extended the Indian concepts of sine and cosine to other trigonometrical ratios, like tangent, secant and their inverse functions. Derived the formula: $\sin \alpha = \tan \alpha / \sqrt{1 + \tan^2 \alpha}$ and $\cos \alpha = 1/\sqrt{1 + \tan^2 \alpha}$.

- ca. 1000 -- AbÅ« Sahl al-QÅ«hÄ« (Kuhi) solves equations higher than the second degree.
- ca. 1000 -- Law of sines is discovered by Muslim mathematicians, but it is uncertain who discovers it first between Abu-Mahmud al-Khujandi, Abu Nasr Mansur, and Abu al-Wafa.
- 1070 -- Omar Khayyám begins to write Treatise on Demonstration of Problems of _____ and classifies cubic equations.
- ca. 1100 -- Omar Khayyám 'gave a complete classification of cubic equations with geometric solutions found by means of intersecting conic sections.' He became the first to find general geometric solutions of cubic equations and laid the foundations for the development of analytic geometry and non-Euclidean geometry. He also extracted roots using the decimal system .
- 1100s -- Bhaskara Acharya writes the 'Bijaganita' , which is the first text that recognizes that a positive number has two square roots
- 1130 -- Al-Samawal gave a definition of _____: '[it is concerned] with operating on unknowns using all the arithmetical tools, in the same way as the arithmetician operates on the known.'
- 1135 -- Sharafeddin Tusi followed al-Khayyam's application of _____ to geometry, and wrote a treatise on cubic equations which 'represents an essential contribution to another _____ which aimed to study curves by means of equations, thus inaugurating the beginning of algebraic geometry.'
- ca. 1250 -- Nasir Al-Din Al-Tusi attempts to develop a form of non-Euclidean geometry.
- 1400s -- Nilakantha Somayaji, a Kerala school mathematician, writes the 'Aryabhatiya Bhasya', which contains work on infinite-series expansions, problems of _____, and spherical geometry

- 1520 -- Scipione dal Ferro develops a method for solving 'depressed' cubic equations (cubic equations without an x^2 term), but does not publish.
- 1535 -- Niccolo Tartaglia independently develops a method for solving depressed cubic equations but also does not publish.
- 1539 -- Gerolamo Cardano learns Tartaglia's method for solving depressed cubics and discovers a method for depressing cubics, thereby creating a method for solving all cubics.
- 1540 -- Lodovico Ferrari solves the quartic equation.

- 1600s - Putumana Somayaji writes the 'Paddhati', which presents a detailed discussion of various trigonometric series
- 1619 - René Descartes discovers analytic geometry (Pierre de Fermat claimed that he also discovered it independently),
- 1619 - Johannes Kepler discovers two of the Kepler-Poinsot polyhedra.
- 1637 - Pierre de Fermat claims to have proven Fermat's Last Theorem in his copy of Diophantus' Arithmetica,
- 1637 - First use of the term imaginary number by René Descartes; it was meant to be derogatory.

- 1722 - Abraham de Moivre states de Moivre's formula connecting trigonometric functions and complex numbers,
- 1733 - Giovanni Gerolamo Saccheri studies what geometry would be like if Euclid's fifth postulate were false,
- 1796 - Carl Friedrich Gauss proves that the regular 17-gon can be constructed using only a compass and straightedge
- 1797 - Caspar Wessel associates vectors with complex numbers and studies complex number operations in geometrical terms,
- 1799 - Carl Friedrich Gauss proves the fundamental theorem of _____.

- 1799 - Paolo Ruffini partially proves the Abel-Ruffini theorem that quintic or higher equations cannot be solved by a general formula,

- 1806 - Louis Poinsot discovers the two remaining Kepler-Poinsot polyhedra.
- 1806 - Jean-Robert Argand publishes proof of the Fundamental theorem of _____ and the Argand diagram,
- 1824 - Niels Henrik Abel partially proves the Abel-Ruffini theorem that the general quintic or higher equations cannot be solved by a general formula involving only arithmetical operations and roots,
- 1829 - Bolyai, Gauss, and Lobachevsky invent hyperbolic non-Euclidean geometry,
- 1832 - Évariste Galois presents a general condition for the solvability of algebraic equations, thereby essentially founding group theory and Galois theory,
- 1837 - Pierre Wantsel proves that doubling the cube and trisecting the angle are impossible with only a compass and straightedge, as well as the full completion of the problem of constructability of regular polygons
- 1843 - William Hamilton discovers the calculus of quaternions and deduces that they are non-commutative,
- 1847 - George Boole formalizes symbolic logic in The Mathematical Analysis of Logic, defining what now is called Boolean _____,
- 1854 - Bernhard Riemann introduces Riemannian geometry,
- 1854 - Arthur Cayley shows that quaternions can be used to represent rotations in four-dimensional space,
- 1858 - August Ferdinand Möbius invents the Möbius strip,
- 1870 - Felix Klein constructs an analytic geometry for Lobachevski's geometry thereby establishing its self-consistency and the logical independence of Euclid's fifth postulate,
- 1873 - Charles Hermite proves that e is transcendental,
- 1878 - Charles Hermite solves the general quintic equation by means of elliptic and modular functions
- 1882 - Ferdinand von Lindemann proves that π is transcendental and that therefore the circle cannot be squared with a compass and straightedge,
- 1882 - Felix Klein invents the Klein bottle,
- 1899 - David Hilbert presents a set of self-consistent geometric axioms in Foundations of Geometry,

- 1901 - Élie Cartan develops the exterior derivative,
- 1905 - Einstein's theory of special relativity.
- 1912 - Luitzen Egbertus Jan Brouwer presents the Brouwer fixed-point theorem,
- 1916 - Einstein's theory of general relativity.
- 1930 - Casimir Kuratowski shows that the three-cottage problem has no solution,
- 1931 - Georges de Rham develops theorems in cohomology and characteristic classes,
- 1933 - Karol Borsuk and Stanislaw Ulam present the Borsuk-Ulam antipodal-point theorem,
- 1955 - H. S. M. Coxeter et al. publish the complete list of uniform polyhedron,
- 1981 - Mikhail Gromov develops the theory of hyperbolic groups, revolutionizing both infinite group theory and global differential geometry,
- 1983 - the classification of finite simple groups, a collaborative work involving some hundred mathematicians and spanning thirty years, is completed,
- 1991 - Alain Connes and John W. Lott develop non-commutative geometry,
- 1998 - Thomas Callister Hales (almost certainly) proves the Kepler conjecture,

- 2003 - Grigori Perelman proves the Poincaré conjecture,
- 2007 - a team of researches throughout North America and Europe used networks of computers to map E8 (mathematics.)

Chapter 14. TRANSFORMATIONS

a. ADHM construction
b. Algebra
c. AA postulate
d. ADE classification

2. In the field of mathematical logic, a clear distinction is made between two notions of axioms: _____ and non-_____

These are certain formulas in a formal language that are universally valid, that is, formulas that are satisfied by every assignment of values. Usually one takes as _____ at least some minimal set of tautologies that is sufficient for proving all tautologies in the language; in the case of predicate logic more _____ than that are required, in order to prove logical truths that are not tautologies in the strict sense.

In propositional logic it is common to take as _____ all formulae of the following forms, where φ, χ, and ψ can be any formulae of the language and where the included primitive connectives are only '¬' for negation of the immediately following proposition and '→' for implication from antecedent to consequent propositions:

1. $\phi \to (\psi \to \phi)$
2. $(\phi \to (\psi \to \chi)) \to ((\phi \to \psi) \to (\phi \to \chi))$
3. $(\neg\phi \to \neg\psi) \to (\psi \to \phi)$.

Each of these patterns is an axiom schema, a rule for generating an infinite number of axioms. For example, if A, B, and C are propositional variables, then $A \to (B \to A)$ and $(A \to \neg B) \to (C \to (A \to \neg B))$ are both instances of axiom schema 1, and hence are axioms.

a. Theorem
b. Logical axioms
c. Contrapositive
d. Logically equivalent

3. In mathematics, the _____ of a real number is its numerical value without regard to its sign. So, for example, 3 is the _____ of both 3 and −3.

The _____ of a number a is denoted by | a |.

a. AA postulate
b. ADHM construction
c. ADE classification
d. Absolute value

4. An injective function is called an injection, and is also said to be a _____ function (not to be confused with _____ correspondence, i.e. a bijective function.)

A function f that is not injective is sometimes called many-to-one. (However, this terminology is also sometimes used to mean 'single-valued', i.e. each argument is mapped to at most one value.)

a. Isometry
b. One-to-one
c. Identity function
d. AA postulate

Chapter 14. TRANSFORMATIONS

5. In geometry, two sets of points are called _____ if one can be transformed into the other by an isometry, i.e., a combination of translations, rotations and reflections. Less formally, two figures are _____ if they have the same shape and size, but are in different positions (for instance one may be rotated, flipped, or simply placed somewhere else).
   a. 11-cell
   b. 1-center problem
   c. -module
   d. Congruent

6. In mathematics, an _____, isometric isomorphism or congruence mapping is a distance-preserving isomorphism between metric spaces. Geometric figures which can be related by an _____ are called congruent.

   They are often used in constructions where one space is embedded in another space. For instance, the completion of a metric space M involves an _____ from M into M', a quotient set of the space of Cauchy sequences on M. The original space M is thus isometrically isomorphic to a subspace of a complete metric space, and it is usually identified with this subspace.

   a. One-to-one
   b. Identity function
   c. AA postulate
   d. Isometry

7. A _____ is a visual representation of an area--a symbolic depiction highlighting relationships between elements of that space such as objects, regions, and themes.

   Many _____s are static two-dimensional, geometrically accurate (or approximately accurate) representations of three-dimensional space, while others are dynamic or interactive, even three-dimensional. Although most commonly used to depict geography, _____s may represent any space, real or imagined, without regard to context or scale; e.g. Brain mapping, DNA mapping, and extraterrestrial mapping.

   a. Map
   b. -module
   c. 11-cell
   d. 1-center problem

8. In mathematics, a _____ is a map that transforms an object into its mirror image. For example, a _____ of the small English letter p in respect to a vertical line would look like q. In order to reflect a planar figure one needs the 'mirror' to be a line , while for _____s in the three-dimensional space one would use a plane for a mirror.
   a. Rotation of axes
   b. Translation
   c. Reflection
   d. Point reflection

9. In mathematics, an _____ on a real vector space is a choice of which ordered bases are 'positively' oriented and which are 'negatively' oriented. In the three-dimensional Euclidean space, the two possible basis _____s are called right-handed and left-handed (or right-chiral and left-chiral), respectively. However, the choice of _____ is independent of the handedness or chirality of the bases (although right-handed bases are typically declared to be positively oriented, they may also be assigned a negative _____.)
   a. Adams-hemisphere-in-a-square
   b. Orientation
   c. Apex
   d. Apollonius' theorem

10. In mathematics, a _____ is a flat surface. _____s can arise as subspaces of some higher dimensional space, as with the walls of a room, or they may enjoy an independent existence in their own right, as in the setting of Euclidean geometry

a. Simple polytope
c. Plane
b. Parallelogram law
d. Pendent

11. In Euclidean geometry, a _____ is moving every point a constant distance in a specified direction. It is one of the rigid motions (other rigid motions include rotation and reflection.) A _____ can also be interpreted as the addition of a constant vector to every point, or as shifting the origin of the coordinate system.
   a. Rotation of axes
   b. Point reflection
   c. Reflection
   d. Translation

12. In geometry, a _____ is a type of isometry of the Euclidean plane: the combination of a reflection in a line and a translation along that line. Reversing the order of combining gives the same result. Depending on context, we may consider a reflection a special case, where the translation vector is the zero vector.
   a. Translation
   b. Glide reflection
   c. Rotation of axes
   d. Point reflection

13. A _____ is a movement of an object in a circular motion. A two-dimensional object rotates around a center (or point) of _____. A three-dimensional object rotates around a line called an axis.
   a. Rotation
   b. Square lattice
   c. Curve of constant width
   d. Similarity

14. _____ is one of the basic operations in mathematical morphology. Originally developed for binary images, it has been expanded first to grayscale images, and then to complete lattices. The _____ operation usually uses a structuring element for probing and expanding the shapes contained in the input image.
   a. Dilation
   b. 11-cell
   c. -module
   d. 1-center problem

15. In geometry, _____ is a polytope operation where facets are separated and moved radially apart, and new facets are formed at separated elements (vertices, edges, etc.) Equivalently this operation can be imagined by keeping facets in the same location, but reducing their size.

According to Coxeter, this multidimensional term was defined by Alicia Boole Stott for creating new polytopes, specifically starting from regular polytopes constructs new uniform polytopes.

   a. ADE classification
   b. ADHM construction
   c. Expansion
   d. AA postulate

16. One of the meanings of the terms _____ and _____ transformation (also called dilation) of a Euclidean space is a function f from the space into itself that multiplies all distances by the same positive scalar r, so that for any two points x and y we have

$$d(f(x), f(y)) = rd(x, y),$$

where 'd(x,y)' is the Euclidean distance from x to y. Two sets are called similar if one is the image of the other under such a _____

Chapter 14. TRANSFORMATIONS

A special case is a homothetic transformation or central _____: it neither involves rotation nor taking the mirror image.

a. Similar
b. Flat
c. Square lattice
d. Similarity

17. In mathematics, computing, linguistics, and related subjects, an _____ is a finite sequence of instructions, an explicit, step-by-step procedure for solving a problem, often used for calculation and data processing. It is formally a type of effective method in which a list of well-defined instructions for completing a task will, when given an initial state, proceed through a well-defined series of successive states, eventually terminating in an end-state. The transition from one state to the next is not necessarily deterministic; some _____s, known as probabilistic _____s, incorporate randomness.

a. ADE classification
b. ADHM construction
c. AA postulate
d. Algorithm

18. A _____ is generally 'a rough or fragmented geometric shape that can be split into parts, each of which is (at least approximately) a reduced-size copy of the whole,' a property called self-similarity. The term was coined by Beno>ît Mandelbrot in 1975 and was derived from the Latin fractus meaning 'broken' or 'fractured.' A mathematical _____ is based on an equation that undergoes iteration, a form of feedback based on recursion.

A _____ often has the following features:

- It has a fine structure at arbitrarily small scales.
- It is too irregular to be easily described in traditional Euclidean geometric language.
- It is self-similar .
- It has a Hausdorff dimension which is greater than its topological dimension (although this requirement is not met by space-filling curves such as the Hilbert curve.)
- It has a simple and recursive definition.

Because they appear similar at all levels of magnification, _____s are often considered to be infinitely complex (in informal terms.) Natural objects that approximate _____s to a degree include clouds, mountain ranges, lightning bolts, coastlines, and snow flakes.

a. Fractal
b. Julia set
c. -module
d. Disjunction

19. In mathematics, a _____ is a convincing demonstration (within the accepted standards of the field) that some mathematical statement is necessarily true. _____s are obtained from deductive reasoning, rather than from inductive or empirical arguments. That is, a _____ must demonstrate that a statement is true in all cases, without a single exception.

a. Theorem
b. Proof
c. Logical axioms
d. Contrapositive

20. In geometry, topology and related branches of mathematics a spatial _____ describes a specific object within a given space that consists of neither volume, area, length, nor any other higher dimensional analogue. Thus, a _____ is a 0-dimensional object. Because of their nature as one of the simplest geometric concepts, they are often used in one form or another as the fundamental constituents of geometry, physics, vector graphics, and many other fields.
- a. -module
- b. 11-cell
- c. 1-center problem
- d. Point

21. A _____ is one of the basic shapes of geometry: a polygon with three corners or vertices and three sides or edges which are line segments. A _____ with vertices A, B, and C is denoted ABC.

In Euclidean geometry any three non-collinear points determine a unique _____ and a unique plane (i.e. a two-dimensional Euclidean space.)

- a. 1-center problem
- b. -module
- c. Triangle
- d. 11-cell

22. _____ generally conveys two primary meanings. The first is an imprecise sense of harmonious or aesthetically-pleasing proportionality and balance; such that it reflects beauty or perfection. The second meaning is a precise and well-defined concept of balance or 'patterned self-similarity' that can be demonstrated or proved according to the rules of a formal system: by geometry, through physics or otherwise.
- a. Symmetry
- b. Crystal system
- c. Tessellation
- d. Screw axis

23. A _____ or tiling of the plane is a collection of plane figures that fills the plane with no overlaps and no gaps. One may also speak of _____ s of the parts of the plane or of other surfaces. Generalizations to higher dimensions are also possible.
- a. Tessellation
- b. Crystal system
- c. Screw axis
- d. Symmetry

24. The _____ of a two-dimensional figure is a line such that, if a perpendicular is constructed, any two points lying on the perpendicular at equal distances from the _____ are identical. Another way to think about it is that if the shape were to be folded in half over the axis, the two halves would be identical: the two halves are each other's mirror image. Thus a square has four axes of symmetry, because there are four different ways to fold it and have the edges all match.
- a. Inscribed sphere
- b. Angle bisectors
- c. Interior angle
- d. Axis of symmetry

25. Discrete _____ come in three types: (1) finite point groups, which include only rotations, reflections, inversion and rotoinversion - they are in fact just the finite subgroups of O(n), (2) infinite lattice groups, which include only translations, and (3) infinite space groups which combines elements of both previous types, and may also include extra transformations like screw axis and glide reflection. There are also continuous _____, which contain rotations of arbitrarily small angles or translations of arbitrarily small distances. The group of all symmetries of a sphere O(3) is an example of this, and in general such continuous _____ are studied as Lie groups.
- a. Corresponding sides
- b. Lateral surface
- c. Sphere
- d. Symmetry Groups

26. 3. A binary function f:A>×A >→ B is said to be _____ if:

Chapter 14. TRANSFORMATIONS

The first known use of the term was in a French Journal published in 1814

Records of the implicit use of the _____ property go back to ancient times. The Egyptians used the _____ property of multiplication to simplify computing products.

a. 1-center problem
b. Commutative
c. 11-cell
d. -module

27. In logic and mathematics, or, also known as logical _____ or inclusive _____ is a logical operator that results in true whenever one or more of its operands are true. E.g. in this context, 'A or B' is true if A is true, or if B is true, or if both A and B are true. In grammar, or is a coordinating conjunction.

a. Fractal
b. -module
c. Disjunction
d. Julia set

28. Induction or _____, sometimes called inductive logic, is reasoning which takes us 'beyond the confines of our current evidence or knowledge to conclusions about the unknown.' The premises of an inductive argument indicate some degree of support (inductive probability) for the conclusion but do not entail it; i.e. they do not ensure its truth. Induction is used to ascribe properties or relations to types based on an observation instance (i.e., on a number of observations or experiences); or to formulate laws based on limited observations of recurring phenomenal patterns. Induction is employed, for example, in using specific propositions such as:

This ice is cold.

a. ADE classification
b. AA postulate
c. Axiom
d. Inductive reasoning

29. A _____ is a mathematical table used in logic--specifically in connection with Boolean algebra, boolean functions, and propositional calculus--to compute the functional values of logical expressions on each of their functional arguments, that is, on each combination of values taken by their logical variables (Enderton 2001.) In particular, _____s can be used to tell whether a propositional expression is true for all legitimate input values, that is, logically valid.

a. 11-cell
b. Truth table
c. 1-center problem
d. -module

30. In logic and mathematics, logical _____ is a logical operator connecting two statements to assert, p if and only if q where p is a hypothesis and q is a conclusion The operator is denoted using a doubleheaded arrow '↔', an equality sign '=', an equivalence sign '≡', or EQV. It is logically equivalent to ∧, or the XNOR boolean operator.

a. Logical axioms
b. Rule of inference
c. Theorem
d. Biconditional

31. In logic and mathematics, _____ is an operation on propositions. For example, in classical logic _____ is normally interpreted by the truth function that takes truth to falsity and vice versa. In intuitionistic logic, according to the Brouwer-Heyting-Kolmogorov interpretation, the _____ of a proposition P is the proposition whose proofs are the refutations of P.

a. 1-center problem
b. 11-cell
c. Negation
d. -module

32. In computer science, _____s, conditional expressions and conditional constructs are features of a programming language which perform different computations or actions depending on whether a programmer-specified condition evaluates to true or false Apart from the case of branch predication, this is always achieved by selectively altering the control flow based on some condition.

In imperative programming languages, the term '_____' is usually used, whereas in functional programming, the terms 'conditional expression' or 'conditional construct' are preferred, because these terms all have distinct meanings.

a. Conditional statement
b. 1-center problem
c. -module
d. 11-cell

33. In vernacular terms, this states 'If P then Q', or, 'If Socrates is a man then Socrates is human.' In a conditional such as this, P is called the antecedent and Q the consequent. One statement is the _____ of the other just when its antecedent is the negated consequent of the other, and vice-versa. The _____ of the given example statement would be:

$$(\neg Q \to \neg P)$$

That is, 'If not-Q then not-P', or more clearly, 'If Q is not the case, then P is not the case.' Using our example, this is rendered 'If Socrates is not human, then Socrates is not a man.' This statement is said to be contraposed to the original, and is logically equivalent to it.

a. Contrapositive
b. Theorem
c. Logically equivalent
d. Logical axioms

34. In logic, _____ is a form of proof that establishes the truth or validity of a proposition by demonstrating the truth or validity of the converse of its negated parts.

In other words, to prove by contraposition that $P \Rightarrow Q$, prove that $\neg Q \Rightarrow \neg P$.

a. Proof by contrapositive
b. 1-center problem
c. -module
d. 11-cell

35. A _____ is an instrument used in geometry, technical drawing and engineering/building to measure distances and/or to rule straight lines. Strictly speaking, the _____ is essentially a straightedge used to rule lines and the calibrated instrument used for determining measurement is called a 'measure'. However, common usage is that a _____ is a calibrated straightedge that can be used for making measurements.

Chapter 14. TRANSFORMATIONS

   a. 11-cell
   c. -module
   b. 1-center problem
   d. Ruler

36. In logic, statements p and q are _____ if they have the same logical content.

Syntactically, p and q are equivalent if each can be proved from the other. Semantically, p and q are equivalent if they have the same truth value in every model.

   a. Contrapositive
   c. Rule of inference
   b. Theorem
   d. Logically equivalent

37. In geometry and trigonometry, an _____ is the figure formed by two rays sharing a common endpoint, called the vertex of the _____ . The magnitude of the _____ is the 'amount of rotation' that separates the two rays, and can be measured by considering the length of circular arc swept out when one ray is rotated about the vertex to coincide with the other Where there is no possibility of confusion, the term '_____' is used interchangeably for both the geometric configuration itself and for its angular magnitude (which is simply a numerical quantity.)

   a. ADE classification
   c. Angle
   b. ADHM construction
   d. AA postulate

38. A _____ is a number that determines the location of a point along some line or curve. A list of two, three, or more _____s can be used to determine the location of a point on a surface, volume, or higher-dimensional domain.

For example, the longitude is a _____ which determines the position of a point along the Earth's equator, and latitude is another _____ that defines a poisition along a meridian.

   a. -module
   c. Coordinate
   b. 1-center problem
   d. 11-cell

39. A _____ is a simple shape of Euclidean geometry consisting of those points in a plane which are the same distance from a given point called the centre. The common distance of the points of a _____ from its center is called its radius.

_____s are simple closed curves which divide the plane into two regions, an interior and an exterior.

   a. Circle
   c. -module
   b. 11-cell
   d. 1-center problem

40. In geometry, the circumscribed circle or circumcircle of a polygon is a circle which passes through all the vertices of the polygon. The center of this circle is called the _____.

A polygon which has a circumscribed circle is called a cyclic polygon.

   a. Nine-Point Circle
   c. Circumscribed
   b. Circular sector
   d. Circumcenter

41. The three altitudes intersect in a single point, called the _____ of the triangle. The _____ lies inside the triangle (and consequently the feet of the altitudes all fall on the triangle) if and only if the triangle is not obtuse (i.e. does not have an angle greater than a right angle.) See also orthocentric system.
   a. ADE classification
   b. Equilateral triangle
   c. AA postulate
   d. Orthocenter

42. In geometry, the incircle or inscribed circle of a triangle is the largest circle contained in the triangle; it touches (is tangent to) the three sides. The center of the incircle is called the triangle's _____.

An excircle or escribed circle of the triangle is a circle lying outside the triangle, tangent to one of its sides and tangent to the extensions of the other two.

   a. Osculating circle
   b. AA postulate
   c. ADE classification
   d. Incenter

43. In geometry, the _____ is a circle that can be constructed for any given triangle. It is so named because it passes through nine significant points, six lying on the triangle itself (unless the triangle is obtuse.) They include:

   - The midpoint of each side of the triangle
   - The foot of each altitude
   - The midpoint of the segment of each altitude from its vertex to the orthocenter (where the three altitudes meet)

The _____ is also known as Feuerbach's circle, Euler's circle, Terquem's circle, the six-points circle, the twelve-points circle, the n-point circle, the medioscribed circle, the mid circle or the circum-midcircle.

   a. Circular sector
   b. Circumcenter
   c. Circle sector
   d. Nine-Point Circle

ANSWER KEY

Chapter 1
1. c	2. c	3. a	4. d	5. d	6. b	7. d	8. c	9. a	10. d
11. d	12. d	13. d	14. b	15. d	16. c	17. b	18. a	19. b	20. b
21. a	22. b	23. d	24. a	25. d	26. c	27. c	28. d	29. b	

Chapter 2
1. d	2. d	3. d	4. d	5. c	6. d	7. d	8. d	9. d	10. d
11. d	12. d	13. d	14. c	15. d	16. c	17. c	18. d	19. c	20. d
21. d	22. c	23. d							

Chapter 3
1. c	2. d	3. d	4. a	5. a	6. d	7. d	8. a	9. d	10. d
11. d	12. b	13. c	14. d	15. d	16. c	17. b	18. d	19. d	20. c
21. d	22. d	23. d	24. d	25. d	26. a	27. d	28. d	29. d	30. d
31. b	32. a	33. d	34. a	35. b	36. c	37. c	38. b	39. d	40. b
41. a	42. c	43. c	44. d						

Chapter 4
1. a	2. b	3. d	4. d	5. c	6. d	7. d	8. d	9. a	10. a
11. d	12. d	13. b	14. d	15. c	16. a	17. b	18. d	19. a	20. a
21. d	22. b	23. d	24. b	25. d	26. b	27. d	28. d	29. b	

Chapter 5
| 1. b | 2. c | 3. d | 4. d | 5. b | 6. d | 7. d | 8. d | 9. b | 10. d |
| 11. b | 12. d | 13. b | 14. d | 15. c | 16. d | 17. d | 18. c | 19. d | 20. d |

Chapter 6
1. c	2. d	3. d	4. a	5. a	6. d	7. d	8. a	9. d	10. d
11. d	12. b	13. d	14. b	15. c	16. d	17. d	18. a	19. b	20. c
21. c	22. c	23. b	24. d	25. d	26. b	27. d	28. d		

Chapter 7
1. c	2. b	3. b	4. b	5. d	6. d	7. d	8. d	9. d	10. a
11. d	12. d	13. c	14. d	15. d	16. c	17. d	18. d	19. d	20. c
21. c	22. b	23. d	24. d	25. a	26. d	27. b	28. c	29. d	30. b
31. b	32. d	33. c	34. c	35. a					

Chapter 8
1. b	2. a	3. b	4. d	5. c	6. c	7. b	8. d	9. a	10. b
11. d	12. d	13. d	14. d	15. d	16. d	17. d	18. c	19. c	20. d
21. a	22. d	23. d	24. d	25. d					

Chapter 9
1. d	2. d	3. a	4. d	5. c	6. c	7. a	8. b	9. c	10. d
11. c	12. c	13. c	14. a	15. a	16. b	17. d	18. a	19. b	20. d
21. a	22. d	23. d	24. d						

Chapter 10

1. d	2. b	3. a	4. d	5. a	6. d	7. d	8. d	9. a	10. d
11. d	12. b	13. a	14. d	15. a	16. d	17. b	18. c	19. d	20. c
21. b	22. a	23. b	24. a	25. b	26. d	27. d	28. c	29. c	30. d
31. d	32. d	33. d	34. d	35. d					

Chapter 11

1. b	2. d	3. c	4. b	5. a	6. d	7. d	8. d	9. d	10. d
11. b	12. d	13. d	14. c	15. d	16. d	17. a	18. d	19. d	20. b
21. d	22. a	23. a	24. a	25. d	26. b	27. b	28. d	29. c	30. d
31. a	32. d	33. d	34. d	35. d	36. b	37. c	38. a		

Chapter 12

1. b	2. d	3. b	4. d	5. c	6. c	7. d	8. d	9. d	10. a
11. d	12. d	13. d	14. c	15. c	16. a	17. b	18. d	19. d	20. c
21. c	22. d	23. d	24. d	25. d	26. d	27. c	28. d	29. d	30. d
31. b									

Chapter 13

1. d	2. d	3. d	4. c	5. b	6. c	7. b	8. d	9. d	10. d
11. d	12. d	13. c	14. a	15. b	16. b	17. d	18. d	19. a	20. a
21. c	22. d	23. c	24. c	25. a	26. d	27. d			

Chapter 14

1. b	2. b	3. d	4. b	5. d	6. d	7. a	8. c	9. b	10. c
11. d	12. b	13. a	14. a	15. c	16. d	17. d	18. a	19. b	20. d
21. c	22. a	23. a	24. d	25. d	26. b	27. c	28. d	29. b	30. d
31. c	32. a	33. a	34. a	35. d	36. d	37. c	38. c	39. a	40. d
41. d	42. d	43. d							